People in prayer
Ten portraits from the Bible

John White

INTER-VARSITY PRESS

INTER-VARSITY PRESS

38 De Montfort Street, Leicester LE1 7GP,
England

First British edition 1978

ISBN 0 85110 401 0

Printed in Great Britain by
Fletcher & Son Ltd, Norwich

Inter-Varsity Press is the publishing division of the
Universities and Colleges Christian Fellowship
(formerly the Inter-Varsity Fellowship), a student
movement linking Christian Unions in universities
and colleges throughout the British Isles, and a
member of the International Fellowship of Evangelical Students. For information about local and
regional activities in Great Britain write to UCCF,
38 De Montfort Street, Leicester LE1 7GP.

To Scott and Kevin

Preface

I have often been helped profoundly by studying and preaching about prayers in the Bible. This is a book about ten specific prayers recorded in the Bible, not about the topic of prayer. I have done this because too many books already exist *about* prayer, and especially about how to pray. What we have lacked was the insight that comes from eavesdropping on some of the most significant prayers in human history. They were recorded for our learning and I felt they were being neglected.

I had always realized that a book about the prayers the Bible records would differ from a book about prayer. Yet I had never realized how profound the difference would prove. When I began, I assumed that in looking at prayers I would learn about prayer. And so I have. But I have learned much more.

If you want to learn about windows, you will do well to take a look at a few of them. The problem will be that you will not only look *at*, you will look *through*. And if your curiosity is anything like mine, the windows themselves will at times disappear.

People in Prayer

Bible prayers are like that. It is what you see through them that matters. For they are windows on eternity, looking out on the profoundest issues of life and death. Before long you forget you are dealing with a prayer, so startled are you by what you see beyond it. From time to time I have had to tap on the glass pane so that I would not forget what I was doing.

It has been difficult to know what prayers to include and which to leave out of this book. It would be impossible (or at least very hard work) to include all the psalms, for instance. In general I have tried to select those prayers in which we know something about the persons who prayed and the circumstances driving them to prayer.

I have omitted some outstanding prayers. For many reasons I left out the Lord's Prayer (books without number have been written on it; it did not arise out of the Lord's personal conflict and so forth). I also omitted his high priestly prayer in John 17, to which I felt unequal. I left out Nehemiah's prayer —which I dearly love—hoping I might be able to devote an entire book to it and all it led to. In any case Daniel's prayer, which I have included, covers almost the same ground.

I have also included things which would hardly be considered suitable in books on prayer. Is dancing ever prayer? David danced before the Lord and so do many people today. I have therefore widened the definition of prayer beyond what some people would consider appropriate, looking at it in the broader sense of a divine-human interaction.

Yet in this sense, just as in the narrower sense of the term prayer, the lesson that has become more basic to my thinking than any other is that prayer begins and ends with God. It is the thrust of my opening chapters and a theme, I hope, that links the book together, making it a whole. To me the adventure of preparing this book has been one of growing more deeply aware of who and what God is. If you can gain from reading it what I have gained from writing it, we shall both be blessed.

1

**Genesis
18:9-33**

They said to him, "Where is Sarah your wife?" And
he said, "She is in the tent." The LORD said, "I will
surely return to you in the spring, and Sarah your wife
shall have a son." And Sarah was listening at the tent
door behind him. Now Abraham and Sarah were old,
advanced in age; it had ceased to be with Sarah after
the manner of women. So Sarah laughed to herself,
saying, "After I have grown old, and my husband is
old, shall I have pleasure?" The LORD said to
Abraham, "Why did Sarah laugh, and say, 'Shall I
indeed bear a child, now that I am old?' Is anything too
hard for the LORD? At the appointed time I will
return to you, in the spring, and Sarah shall have a
son." But Sarah denied, saying, "I did not laugh"; for
she was afraid. He said, "No, but you did laugh."

Then the men set out from there, and they looked
toward Sodom; and Abraham went with them to set
them on their way. The LORD said, "Shall I hide from
Abraham what I am about to do, seeing that Abraham
shall become a great and mighty nation, and all the
nations of the earth shall bless themselves by him? No,
for I have chosen him, that he may charge his children
and his household after him to keep the way of the
LORD by doing righteousness and justice; so that the
LORD may bring to Abraham what he has promised
him." Then the LORD said, "Because the outcry
against Sodom and Gomorrah is great and their sin is
very grave, I will go down to see whether they have

done altogether according to the outcry which has come to me; and if not, I will know."

So the men turned from there, and went toward Sodom; but Abraham still stood before the LORD. Then Abraham drew near, and said, "Wilt thou indeed destroy the righteous with the wicked? Suppose there are fifty righteous within the city; wilt thou then destroy the place and not spare it for the fifty righteous who are in it? Far be it from thee to do such a thing, to slay the righteous with the wicked, so that the righteous fare as the wicked! Far be that from thee! Shall not the Judge of all the earth do right?" And the LORD said, "If I find at Sodom fifty righteous in the city, I will spare the whole place for their sake." Abraham answered, "Behold, I have taken upon myself to speak to the Lord, I who am but dust and ashes. Suppose five of the fifty righteous are lacking? Wilt thou destroy the whole city for lack of five?" And he said, "I will not destroy it if I find forty-five there." Again he spoke to him, and said, "Suppose forty are found there." He answered, "For the sake of forty I will not do it." Then he said, "Oh let not the Lord be angry, and I will speak. Suppose thirty are found there." He answered, "I will not do it, if I find thirty there." He said, "Behold, I have taken upon myself to speak to the Lord. Suppose twenty are found there." He answered, "For the sake of twenty I will not destroy it." Then he said, "Oh let not the Lord be angry, and I will speak again but this once. Suppose ten are found there." He answered, "For the sake of ten I will not destroy it." And the LORD went his way, when he had finished speaking to Abraham; and Abraham returned to his place.

ABRAHAM:
THE DAY
GOD
GREW LARGER

UNLIKE MANY OF US, ABRAHAM had no problem making contact with heaven. He never needed to try. Throughout his long life it was God who made contact with Abraham.

We are not always told exactly how God did so. Often we read, "The Lord said to Abraham, . . ." with no explanation whether God spoke in an audible voice or in the stillness of Abraham's heart. One time God spoke in a vision (Gen. 15:1); on another occasion he "appeared" to Abraham (Gen. 17:1). The important point to grasp is that each time communion between the two is mentioned, God took the initiative. God spoke and Abraham responded. Our prayer lives will be much simpler if the same proves true for us.

And why should it not be so? We think of praying as talking, and certainly talking is involved. But the quality of a conversation may well be determined by the person who initiates it. Indeed our whole reaction to a conversation often depends on who first started it. It is comforting in a group of strangers for somebody to greet us and show a friendly interest. It may on the other hand be difficult for us to start a conversation, and it becomes doubly so when our attempt is met with a cold stare.

God is always speaking. To hear his voice is not usually a mystical experience. It consists merely of a willingness to pay heed to the God who lays a claim on our lives. It is as Hallesby once pointed out "to let Jesus come into our hearts." For the word *hear* in the New Testament does not commonly refer to an auditory experience. More often it means "to pay heed." "There's none so deaf," we used to say in the north of England, "as them as *won't* hear."

Abraham, then, was not unique. God approaches all of us in the same way. To hear him involves no exercise in "tuning in to the right frequency" so much as a humble recognition that it is his prerogative to speak and our responsibility to respond. We may not have such dramatic experiences as Abraham, but remember that Abraham had no knowledge of God from Scripture. He had never read a chapter of the Bible.

Abraham's Guests

Once we are given a vivid picture of what happened when God appeared to him. Three men, probably dressed like Bedouin tribesmen, approached Abraham's encampment during the shimmering noonday heat. Abraham watched their approach, rose to his feet and went forward to greet them.

There is no indication in the narrative that at that point he suspected who his guests were. As the men sat down in the shade of the terebinth trees Abraham hurried to give orders for water to wash his guests' feet and for a large meal to be prepared for them. He was showing them the deferential welcome that desert custom demanded. This same eagerness to please would have been shown to any visitor.

Later, again according to custom, Abraham himself waited

on them. When did he first begin to suspect their identity? It is hard to know. Did they converse during the meal? Did Abraham tell them about his wife Sarah and about her barrenness? The narrative does not tell us. Yet it is unlikely that he would share his highest hopes and deepest shame with men he did not know. Who would? Sarah herself had little faith in Abraham's contact with God or in any promise of an heir.

So if Abraham had not mentioned Sarah's name, it would be startling to hear his guests demand, "Where is Sarah your wife?" His heart would leap suffocatingly as one of the three, who is identified as "the stranger" said, "About this time next year I will be sure to come back to you, and Sarah will have a son."

His legs would shake and he would catch his breath. All his life he had longed for a son and had believed God for one. He had struggled for years against a sense of hopelessness which all but extinguished his faith. And now again the promise came.

Then from the tent sounded Sarah's mocking laughter. What followed must have been frightening to Sarah and Abraham alike. "The stranger" (now referred to in the narrative as "the Lord") rebuked Sarah for her laughter. From behind the sheltering curtains Sarah quickly denied that she had laughed. "No, but you did laugh," came the stern reply.

The embarrassment of the succeeding moments is left to our imaginations. In a dreamlike sequence "the men" are described as looking toward Sodom and Abraham as accompanying them at the start of their journey. (Exactly who are they? One of them clearly represents God revealed in the flesh. Do we here see the members of the Trinity? No. The Holy Spirit is never represented in human form. Moreover the two "men" are later described as angelic beings.)

God's Confidant
Then in one of the most astonishing passages of Scripture we

overhear a divine soliloquy. God is depicted as walking and thinking as a man walks and thinks. We know, of course, that God's thought processes are beyond human comprehension. The God who in the same instant upholds galaxies by his controlling power, who numbers the hairs on your own head and watches every sparrow fall, does not "think" in the limited sense that we ourselves do. Yet it is as if his whole attention is for the moment absorbed with Abraham. "Shall I hide from Abraham what I am about to do?" he asks himself.

Evidently the Lord is about to destroy Sodom in a stroke of catastrophic judgment. Though the evil of the little city trumpets its challenge throughout God's universe, he assures Abraham that his personal and intimate acquaintance with the situation is a prerequisite of justice.

Why should God bother to take Abraham into his confidence? He seems to feel a sense of obligation toward Abraham. Why? If you think about it for a moment you will realize the stupendous implication of the story. The Lord of far-flung galaxies, the Creator of life and of all that exists, the All-Powerful, the All-Knowing, the Inscrutable, the Judge of angels, demons and people is taking the trouble to explain his actions to an individual, and is talking to him without condescension, but in terms that he can understand. In this soliloquy he gives his reason for doing so.

God knew Abraham. He knew that Abraham would order his household in a godly fashion. He knew Abraham would instruct his children properly. Is God then selecting a superior human, one with whom he can have dealings, as distinct from the rest of us? The question is an important one. If we answer, "Yes," then we must face a long struggle to upgrade our lives enough so God would feel it worth his while to share things with us.

"For I know [Abraham]." The word *know* in Hebrew can be translated "chosen" or "made . . . my friend." In saying he knows Abraham, God is saying, "I chose Abraham to be my friend. I have changed the relationship of Creator to creature, of Judge to sinner and have added a new dimension to it. I have selected this man to be my friend. I also want him as a partner. He will have a role in my plans. Moreover, though I know he will keep my precepts and teach them to his children, I want him to be more than a yes man. I want him to be a true partner, sharing fully in those projects he will have a part in."

It may seem inconceivable that the same God wants such a relationship with you. You are a creature he made. You are a sinner he redeemed. You are even his child by adoption and by supernatural new birth. Yet he calls you to a higher dignity —to that of friend and partner. "No longer do I call you servants," Jesus told his disciples, "for the servant does not know what his master is doing; but I have called you friends, for all that I have heard from my Father I have made known to you" (Jn. 15:15). He *chose* you to be such.

Two facts necessarily follow. If you are his friend, he will share his thoughts and plans with you. If you are his partner, he will be concerned about your views on his plans and projects. Whatever else prayer may be, it is intended to be a sharing and a taking counsel with God on matters of importance to him. God has called you to attend a celestial board meeting to deliberate with him on matters of destiny.

You can see at once how this raises the whole level of prayer. It is not intended primarily to be centered in my petty needs and woes. To be sure, God is interested in them. They have a place on his agenda. But the agenda itself has been drawn up in heaven and deals with matters of greatest consequence.

God then is taking counsel with Abraham about the destiny of Sodom. No longer are they discussing a son for Abraham. That matter had already been dismissed summarily. "About this time next year. . . ." God had settled the issue and nothing remained to be said. Now he moves on to a matter which lies beyond the scope of Abraham's personal concerns, and as Abraham looks at the agenda he is flooded with dismay.

People in Prayer

For one thing the stupendous horror of the coming judgment sickened him. To us Sodom means nothing—a city lost in remote history. But to Abraham it meant living people, warm of flesh and quick of movement. It meant slaves and their masters, tradesmen, craftsmen, parents, children, merchants, animals, provisions, houses, gardens. It was in Sodom that his relative Lot lived. He knew Sodom. He had met its king. He had personally rescued many of its citizens when disaster in war had overtaken them (Gen. 14). God had enabled him to deliver the city from the ravages of defeat, yet now he was proposing to obliterate the city and all its inhabitants.

It could not have been only his concern for Lot that sparked the intensity of Abraham's prayer. Had his concern been only for Lot and his family, Abraham would not have stopped short of pleading that the city be saved if ten righteous people could be found in it. No. Abraham had wider concerns than his own family. He was concerned for other people in Sodom.

People differ. Not everyone in Sodom was equally corrupt. There were presumably merciful people there, people of reasonably good will. Abraham's heart reached out in pleading for them. Was God planning to destroy *everybody*?

A strange blend of terror and boldness characterizes his prayer. It was not the "Save-Sodom-if-it-be-your-will. Amen" kind. Whatever else we may say about it, it was a real-issues, facts-and-figures kind of prayer. Abraham knew God meant what he said. Abraham also sensed that if God could be induced to make a promise, God would keep that promise. His whole life had been devoted to learning such a lesson. Yet it was his first board meeting and he was terrified of the Chairman.

What about our "if-it-be-your-will" prayers? Are they biblical? "Thy will be done, on earth as it is in heaven" we repeat in absent-minded solemnity. Prayer does indeed have to do with accomplishing God's will. You are called into prayer

either that you might collaborate with him in bringing his will
to pass or that you might get a larger vision of what he is like.
The phrase "if it be thy will" is more often than not a cop-out.
It means I don't have to come to grips with God. I need not
bother to find out what God's will is. Nor do I have to exercise
faith in the character of the Invisible One who works miracu-
lously in the face of impossible odds. "If it be thy will" is lazy
pseudoreverence, which when translated into Spanish comes
out "*lo que será, será.*"

Terrified though he may be, Abraham wants to get the facts
straight. Yet his prayer is not, as some scholars suggest, a mere
reflection of bargaining practices among traders in the East.
Abraham has nothing to offer in trade with God. Moreover
the stakes are too high. He is not haggling with God. He is desperate to understand.

God stands before Abraham, waiting for his response.
(There is good evidence that such was the original order of
words at the end of verse 22.) And as Abraham steps forward
to speak, we see his perplexity lies not only with the horror of
God's judgment, but with the apparent injustice of it.

"God, How Could You Be Like That?"

"Wilt thou indeed destroy the righteous with the wicked? . . .
Far be that from thee! Shall not the Judge of all the earth do
right?" The foundation of Abraham's very life is being destroyed. If there is one thing he has built his life on, it is the
justice and the faithfulness of the God he has learned to serve.
With dismay he sees standing before him a God he no longer
understands. God has become alien to him. The change in
their relationship threatens to destroy it altogether. It would
have been more comfortable to go on as God's servant and not
as his friend. Who would have thought that God would turn
out to be a monster?

Struggling inside him are painfully conflicting emotions—
his terror of the Almighty and his yearning that the same

17

Almighty be all Abraham longs for him to be. In the end it is his yearning that God shall be just that wins out over his terror. "Suppose there are fifty righteous. . . ."

You cannot have a relationship with God without standing, at one time or another, precisely where Abraham stood. I stood there late one night as I grappled with the apparent injustice of a God who chose Jacob and rejected Esau. I stood there another time as in my morning devotions I read of God's deadly anger against Uzzah whose only fault had been to reach out to prevent the ark of the covenant from tumbling off a cart (2 Sam. 6:6). I was in the middle of a student evangelistic campaign at the time. I remember kneeling on the boards of an old church hall, begging God to show me that he was not the God of 2 Samuel 6. How could I preach of his saving mercy if he were in fact a petulant tyrant?

God has never defended himself when I have come to him in my perplexity. I can well understand Abraham's torment, for it is a torment I have felt. I loved God and wanted him to go on being the God I had always known. I was frightened both by what I seemed to be seeing, and by my own temerity in daring to question the Judge of the universe. Yet with tears and sweat the question had to come, "Lord, how could you *be* like that?" And his answer has always been to show me more of himself than I had seen before, so that my tears and perplexity gave place to awe and to worship.

The same process was taking place between God and Abraham. It is not the fate of Sodom that is the issue in Abraham's prayer, but the character of God. It is easy enough to plead for the doomed and the lost, but it is another matter altogether to question God about his own integrity.

"Behold, I have taken upon myself to speak to the Lord, I who am but dust and ashes." Abraham was painfully aware of the incongruity, the total inappropriateness of what he was doing. Yet without such an awareness what is prayer but a parroting of words? If we close our minds to everything about

God that makes us uncomfortable, we are going through empty motions when we pray. We pray to a god we have ourselves fashioned for our comfort and not to God as he is. True prayer is to respond to the true God as he reveals more of himself by his Spirit in his Word. Prayer defined in such terms can be a terrifying experience. "Woe is me! For I am lost," cried Isaiah (Is. 6:5) as the true God shone through the smoke before him.

So far Abraham has not dared to ask what he really wanted to know. The apparent haggling, the step by step descent in fives and tens is the terrified progress of one who feared lest every step forward should prove his last. "Oh let not the Lord be angry, and I will speak." His fear and his longing are equally apparent. "Oh let not the Lord be angry, and I will speak again but this once. . . ."

Why did Abraham stop at ten? We may never know. One thing is certain. He was reassured. As each response came back at him, "For the sake of forty I will not do it. . . . I will not do it, if I find thirty there. . . . For the sake of ten I will not destroy it, . . ." the image of God was changing in Abraham's eyes. It was no monster that faced him but the familiar God of the covenant. Yet somehow God was larger. He was less comprehensible. And, paradoxically, he was a God Abraham understood better than ever before. A familiar God whom yet he scarcely knew. A righteous God whose judgments were past finding out.

Abraham was satisfied. He did not need to drop his figure any lower. Whether Sodom was consumed or not, the universe was on a solid footing. The storm might be terrible and its havoc beyond belief. Yet all was well.

Abraham had grown into a larger man with a greater God. Prayer had changed him. God's purpose of inviting him to the board meeting had been accomplished. The Chairman himself drew the meeting to a close and left Abraham to the wonder of his new discovery.

2

Genesis 32:22-32

The same night he arose and took his two wives, his two maids, and his eleven children, and crossed the ford of the Jabbok. He took them and sent them across the stream, and likewise everything that he had. And Jacob was left alone; and a man wrestled with him until the breaking of the day. When the man saw that he did not prevail against Jacob, he touched the hollow of his thigh; and Jacob's thigh was put out of joint as he wrestled with him. Then he said, "Let me go, for the day is breaking." But Jacob said, "I will not let you go, unless you bless me." And he said to him, "What is your name?" and he said, "Jacob." Then he said, "Your name shall no more be called Jacob, but Israel, for you have striven with God and with men, and have prevailed." Then Jacob asked him, "Tell me, I pray, your name." But he said, "Why is it that you ask my name?" And there he blessed him. So Jacob called the name of the place Peniel, saying, "For I have seen God face to face, and yet my life is preserved." The sun rose upon him as he passed Penuel, limping because of his thigh. Therefore to this day the Israelites do not eat the sinew of the hip which is upon the hollow of the thigh, because he touched the hollow of Jacob's thigh on the sinew of the hip.

JACOB:

A CRIPPLING
IN THE
CHASM

THE PICTURE OF JACOB WRESTLING one lonely night with the God-man in the gorge of the Jabbok has fired the imaginations of poets and mystics down through the ages. Many see it as a heroic struggle in which Jacob, crippled and exhausted, overcomes the divine resistance to his longings and succeeds in extracting what he wants from God. It becomes the model of prevailing prayer and presents us with the challenge: Who among us will wrestle in prayer as Jacob wrestled and prevail as Jacob prevailed? Prevail over God?

Before we are carried away let us look at what the narrative actually tells us. Let us ask why there was any struggle at all. If God is almighty and man feeble, why is Jacob not immediately overwhelmed? Does God need to cripple Jacob? Does a mouse wrestle with an elephant? Would an elephant even be concerned if a mouse were to strive with it?

The first thing we should notice about the story is that Jacob is not the aggressor. The wording is quite clear. "A man wrestled with [Jacob]." Now if a man hits you, you have two choices. You may hit him back or you may run away. If on the other hand a man wrestles with you, you have no such choice. Whether you wish to flee or to fight back, you are obliged to wrestle too. You struggle either to break away from his grip or to teach him a lesson. Jacob did not wrestle because he chose to but because he was obliged to. The "man" was trying to throw him to the ground.

The problem of why God would bother to strive at all is an awesome one. He has, as it were, reduced himself to Jacob's size. He refuses to take unfair advantage of a weaker opponent. At least he does so until he sees plainly that Jacob has no intention of giving in.

What does it all mean? It means that Jacob had been struggling against God all his life. The conflict by the Jabbok symbolizes his lifelong struggle. His early life had led down to this point, and the rest of his life would ascend from it. Up to this crisis his life has been a long endeavor to resist God's goodness. As is so often the case, it had been a struggle against a God who was determined to bless and to help him.

The Struggle Begins

Rebekah, Jacob's mother, apparently had a rough pregnancy. The movement inside her uterus was not "the fluttering of a bird in the hand" but a vigorous tussle. "The children struggled together within her." The struggle seemed to be a forewarning of something to come and Rebekah, frightened about what was happening to her, went "to inquire of the LORD." She was told, "Two nations are in your womb, and two peoples, born of you, shall be divided; the one shall be stronger than the other, the elder shall serve the younger" (Gen. 25:22-23).

The first twin, Esau, emerged red and hairy, destined to be a hunter, strong in body, impulsive. The second was Jacob, following Esau quickly down the birth canal where "his hand had taken hold of Esau's heel" (Gen. 25:26). Coming events seemed to have cast their shadow before them. The intra-uterine struggle, the hand that grasped the heel of Esau seemed to be curious confirmations of the prophecy. Smooth and subtle, Jacob might be the younger, but he would hang on until the very end to get what he wanted.

As the boys grew older the promise to Jacob seemed unlikely to ever be fulfilled. Esau was a man's man. He was robust and the smell of the fields hung around him. He was also his father Isaac's favorite. He thus had three factors going for him. As the older of the two he had the birthright: a greater claim on the inheritance and automatic seniority in the family hierarchy. Physically he was Jacob's superior. And as his father's favorite he was the likely candidate of Isaac's blessing, a prophetic utterance that the patriarchs made on their death-beds concerning their sons.

Jacob surely must have realized all this. But he also must have known from his mother about the promise God had made. Yet neither Rebekah nor Jacob took the promise seriously enough. It was as though they extracted from it the feeling that Jacob had the *right* to supremacy over Esau, but both of them lacked trust that God would give what he had promised. If, then, Jacob was to get his due, it was to be by playing on Esau's weaknesses, by deception and by superstition. In these ways he struggled half his life to gain for himself the things God had planned to give him anyway. In the end he gained exactly what God had promised (but no more). Tragically he had missed, in the struggle, the peace and the fellowship with God he might otherwise have enjoyed. God had wanted him to have the inheritance plus peace and fellowship with himself. Instead Jacob had twenty-one years of anxiety.

So when Esau, strong in body but weak in self-denial, came in one day faint with hunger to smell the fragrance of Jacob's cooking, Jacob was able to extract from him the promise of his birthright in exchange for a bowl of lentil soup. Jacob seized his chance.

"First sell me your birthright," he demanded. This was a violation of Bedouin custom. When a man is faint and starving, you feed him. He may be a perfect stranger, but your duty is to help him survive. And if that man is your twin brother. . . .

"I am about to die," came Esau's self-pitying reply. "Of what use is a birthright to me?"

But Jacob was not satisfied. "Swear to me first," he insisted. And Esau swore. The bargain was sealed. For the price of a bowl of soup Jacob had purchased the coveted seniority. It was his first step toward gaining supremacy. But much more was to follow.

Primitive peoples are better able than some of us to be alert to the onset of death. The patriarchs, as death approached, would lay their hands on their offspring and "bless" them, that is to say, make a prophetic utterance about the life of the child at hand. There was no doubt in the mind of Rebekah that when her husband Isaac would bless his two sons, Esau would get the better deal. So when the time came for action, she was ready.

One day Isaac, blind and sensing that his death was now approaching, sent Esau to hunt. If he was to give the patriarchal blessing he would give it from a full stomach. But Rebekah and Jacob tricked the old man. She prepared the sort of dish Isaac was expecting, dressed Jacob in Esau's clothing, covered his smooth neck with goatskin and sent him into his father to receive the blessing that was to have been Esau's (Gen. 27:1-40).

The story is a pitiful one, and our sympathies fly more readily to the deceived old man. All four of them, Isaac, Rebekah, Esau and Jacob, shared utter confidence in the power of the words spoken. The blessing pronounced over Jacob, a blessing predicting that he would be "lord over [his] brothers," was to them as solid an acquisition as the title deed to a piece of land. What had been done, even by deception, could not be undone. There was no court of appeal. Esau's rage and sorrow were bitter.

Thus Jacob (whose name meant "supplanter") lived up to his name a second time. More important, he again won by human effort what God had all along intended to give him. It is curious that for years afterward Jacob continued to follow this same futile pattern, struggling to win what he could have had freely.

Neither Peace nor Protection

Because of Esau's rage, it became unwise for Jacob to stay at home. He was sent off by his parents on the pretext of seeking a wife. Soon after he set out he experienced his first encounter with God.

As he slept one night under the open sky with a flat stone for a pillow, he dreamed he saw a ladder by which angels made their journeys to and from heaven. The Lord stood beside him and made an astonishing series of promises.

First he assured Jacob that the territory for hundreds of miles around was to be given to his descendants. Widening the promise still further he told Jacob that the whole world was to be blessed through those same descendants (Gen. 28: 14). And to reassure him as to the perils that faced him, both imaginary and real, he guaranteed his presence and personal protection until Jacob returned safely home.

Jacob was awed and a little scared when he awoke. In oriental style he made a small pillar out of the stone on which his head had rested, poured oil over it and gave the place a name, Bethel, meaning "the house of God." He also swore an oath, an oath more interesting for what he did not swear than for what he did.

If God would bring him back safely, *then* God would become Jacob's God, and Jacob would devote a tenth of his wealth to him. It was reassuring (albeit terrifying) to be told God would do so much for him. But it would be unwise to count too heavily on the promise. We have no way of assessing Jacob's chain of reasoning. It may never have occurred to him that to doubt the integrity of the most high God was sinful. What is clear is that he was adopting a wait-and-see attitude to the promises. And from his subsequent actions it was plain that he would help the promises along by every device he could think of.

There was a time when I felt myself to be infinitely Jacob's spiritual superior in this regard. "Had God appeared to *me* in a vision and given *me* such promises, . . ." I would think rather smugly. Yet as I look at the matter more realistically I have little room for boasting. I have behind me an infinitely richer and more detailed tradition in the ways of God than Jacob had. I may not have had God speak to me in a dream, but I have scriptural promises by the thousand. Moreover I have on numerous occasions experienced God's dramatic intervention in my life in response to prayer.

Yet even with this apparent advantage I confess that I catch myself at times reacting pretty much as Jacob did. Immediately following some particularly striking answer to prayer, I have no problems. In the glowing aftermath I am full of praise and find it relatively easy to count on God. But as time passes, a curtain of unreality begins to intervene between me and past events, or between me and the Word of God. My praises begin to sound hollow, my declaration of trust in his power and faithfulness a little forced.

In any case, how is one supposed to act in the face of God's promises? "God helps those who help themselves," I am told. Perhaps it is no sign of unbelief to work actively to secure the answer to my prayers.

Everything depends, of course, on my motive for doing so. Do I work because I am counting on God? Or do I do so because I might as well make sure of securing what I want? There is an activity that springs from faith, and another that arises from lack of it.

Jacob: A Crippling in the Chasm

In Jacob's case we know which we are dealing with. Jacob himself makes no bones about his lack of faith. "If . . . and if . . . and if" characterize his response to God.

When you ask God for something, you must be as honest with yourself as Jacob was. When you know the will of God, that is, when the matter clearly exemplifies a basic promise of Scripture, you must ask yourself whether your behavior is the behavior of a person who is counting on God's faithfulness and power, or whether it is that of someone who feels that a little extra insurance will do no harm.

Jacob met his match in trickery when he joined his relative Laban. Having worked seven years to win Rachel, Laban's younger daughter, he was enraged to waken from the drunken stupor of his wedding night to discover that he had not been married to his true love, but to Leah, her unattractive older sister. But Jacob learned his lesson well. He waited years to outsmart Laban.

He loved Rachel enough to accept her as his second wife "on credit" for seven more years of servitude. The story is a sordid one involving jealousies and superstition. And as Laban and Jacob subsequently entered a second phase in their relationship, during which Jacob was allowed to accumulate his own herds in payment of services rendered, Jacob made sure by using every trick he knew that he would get a good bargain.

His life could hardly have been a happy one. He worked like a slave. The constant rivalries of his wives forced him into behavior that was more like that of a male prostitute than a contented husband (Gen. 30:14-16). The working arrangement he had with Laban must have been a source of constant anxiety. (For instance, Jacob had to make good any losses in Laban's flocks from his own herds.)

The contract between the two called for a division of herds by their appearance: the black sheep plus the striped and spotted goats going to Jacob, and the rest to Laban. Each then did his utmost to swindle or outwit the other (Gen. 30:30-43). Jacob even stooped to superstitious practices. He could hardly have enjoyed peace of mind. In fact it is plain that as time passed he grew afraid for his safety.

The whole point about a relationship with God is not what one gains in personal safety or material prosperity but in fellowship with him and peace of mind. You can be perfectly safe yet experience no peace at all. Did Jacob but know it, he was safe. God had no intention of allowing Laban to hurt him (Gen. 31:24). God also was going to see to it that Jacob returned home a wealthy man. But Jacob enjoyed neither the peace that God's protection could have given him nor the sweetness of his fellowship. He was a man haunted by greed, by terror and by a troubled family life.

The Wolf's Bared Throat

In the end he sneaked away from Laban, taking his family, his servants and his flocks with him.

But a greater fear awaited him. Word reached him that Esau, his brother, and four hundred men were on their way to meet him.

In his terror Jacob refused to give way to panic. Feeling that his only hope lay in appeasing Esau and in playing on his sentimentality, Jacob rearranged his flocks and his family, marshaling them as a general would arrange an army. First Esau would be met by servants bringing waves of presents to "my lord Esau" from "your servant Jacob." Later Jacob's wives and children would approach. He would use psychology on his brother.

Ethologists have observed that when a younger wolf challenges the leader of the pack and loses, the younger wolf will present his bared throat to the teeth of his leader. At this point the victor's aggression seems to melt away. Instead of killing his opponent he turns around to urinate while the vanquished wolf sneaks away to lick his wounds.

Jacob: A Crippling in the Chasm

In sending his wives and little ones before him, Jacob was presenting his throat to Esau. After crossing the Jabbok, he found himself alone in the night, anxiously awaiting the outcome. It was then and there that God began dealing with him so forcefully.

So far I have maintained that the struggle between Jacob and the Lord should not be painted as Jacob striving to win something from God. The distinction is important. If you approach God with the determination to pray through a request, as though success in prayer depends upon your determined efforts, you are likely to wind up deeply discouraged.

A good deal depends of course on how one interprets the expression *pray through*. To some people it means to wait for God that one might find clarity in the midst of confusion, an understanding of his outlook, a changed perspective. Such praying through can only be good. This was the sort of thing that Abraham did over the judgment of Sodom.

But to other people *praying through* means forcing your way against resistance until you get through to God. It means battering your bleeding knuckles against the portals of heaven until you gain access. If this kind of praying through were merely an exercise in futility or masochism, it would not be so bad. However, in practice it not only discourages the person who prays, sometimes driving him to despair, it also dishonors God.

Someone might say to me, "Yes, but is it not true that the powers of darkness resist our prayers and that we may need to overcome satanic opposition?" Well, they might have a point; but before digressing I must emphasize that Jacob was not wrestling with Satan, he was wrestling with God.

I can only recall one instance in Scripture where demonic opposition impeded an answer to prayer You can read about it in Daniel 10. I think it is naive to compare ourselves with Daniel, that great prayer warrior. In any case, Daniel was not battering his way through to God's presence. He was not involved with any kind of battle. He was simply so overwhelmed with sorrow that for three weeks he mourned and fasted. The battle that was going on was being fought in heavenly places. Daniel was not fighting it. Nor is it possible to work up the state of mind which overwhelmed Daniel. He mourned and fasted because he could not help doing so. His state of mind was God-produced. Therefore if you must engage in prayerful shadowboxing, don't quote Daniel or Jacob as your excuse.

It is always wrong to work up some kind of state of pseudo-fervor. It is carnal. It is self-defeating. It will get you nowhere. Its end result will either be spiritual pride or profound discouragement. From this arises another principle. Where you do not experience profound emotion in prayer, ignore your emotions. Faith is an attitude of will which says, "Whether I feel that God is there or not, whether I feel he will heed me or not, his Word tells me he hears and answers and I am going to count on that."

Conquered by Dependency

Jacob wrestled with God because he had no choice. He was defending himself, not attacking. Yet the end of the narrative states that he had won a victory. "Your name shall no more be called Jacob," he was told, "but Israel, for you have striven with God and with men, and have prevailed" (Gen. 32:28).

The name *Israel* means "God strove." So far so good. We can rest assured that if God strove then God was indeed the initiator of the struggle.

In what sense then did Jacob prevail? Read the narrative again. Picture the wrestling as God seeking to help Jacob understand something. Picture him as urging upon Jacob truths that Jacob was unwilling to see. Picture him, as they struggle, trying to convince Jacob that he means him no harm, that his intentions are not malicious but merciful. (Often I have had to seize delirious patients as they rush terrified into the Canadian snow. I am the aggressor, yet my purpose is merciful.)

Jacob: A Crippling in the Chasm

But Jacob is too afraid. All his life he has learned one lesson: It is safe to trust no one. Jacob must fight his own battles. So he wrestles on, terrified by unyielding. Then, suddenly—incredible pain and a useless leg.

Have you ever tried wrestling with lumbago or a slipped disc? If you should ever find yourself in Jacob's situation, let me tell you what you will do. You will cling. You will hang onto your opponent with desperation. Either you cling or you fall.

And through the fog of pain and terror the words begin to penetrate Jacob's brain, "Let me go, for the day is breaking."

Let him go? How can he? He isn't even sure whether he can walk. Let him go? How dare he? At some point the awful knowledge has gripped him that the one on whose breast he leans sweating and gasping is the God of his fathers, who could slay him with a glance. And for once, since he has no choice, no other hope, Jacob's tenacity is turned in the right direction.

"I will not let you go, unless you bless me."

They are words God has waited over forty years to hear. He would have preferred that Jacob recognize his helplessness and cast himself on the mercy of his God long before. He did not wish to reduce him to such an extremity, but Jacob left him little choice. And God's response is swift in coming. Jacob had conquered by his helpless dependency.

Is God wrestling with you? If so, what makes you resist? Greed? (He wants to give you of his bounty.) Fear? (He alone can free you of it.) You *must* play it your way just this once? (You are a fool.)

He does not wish to bring you to some extremity in which you have no choice but to cast yourself on his mercy. Yet he will if he has to. Already he may have done so. You must have heard the words of the foolish old lady, "Well, I guess there's nothing left to do now but to trust the Lord!" Trust should come first, not last. Yet there is no limit to what he will do, no desperation he will withhold to teach you this basic lesson in prayer: You are helpless and you have no hope except in him.

The "man" had disappeared, and Jacob stood uncertainly, panting, gently testing his painful leg to see if he could walk. "I have seen God face to face." The words repeated themselves wonderingly through his brain, infusing new life in his exhausted body. *Peniel* ("God's face") he called the place. As he began haltingly and painfully to climb out of the chasm, the rising sun broke over him. After that things would never again be quite the same.

3

And the LORD said to Moses, "I have seen this people, and behold, it is a stiff-necked people; now therefore let me alone, that my wrath may burn hot against them and I may consume them; but of you I will make a great nation."

But Moses besought the LORD his God, and said, "O LORD, why does thy wrath burn hot against thy people, whom thou hast brought forth out of the land of Egypt with great power and with a mighty hand? Why should the Egyptians say, 'With evil intent did he bring them forth, to slay them in the mountains, and to consume them from the face of the earth'? Turn from thy fierce wrath, and repent of this evil against thy people. Remember Abraham, Isaac, and Israel, thy servants, to whom thou didst swear by thine own self, and didst say to them, 'I will multiply your descendants as the stars of heaven, and all this land that I have promised I will give to your descendants, and they shall inherit it for ever.'" And the LORD repented of the evil which he thought to do to his people. . . .

So Moses returned to the LORD and said, "Alas, this people have sinned a great sin; they have made for themselves gods of gold. But now, if thou wilt forgive their sin—and if not, blot me, I pray thee, out of thy book which thou hast written."

. . . Moses said to the LORD, "See, thou sayest to me, 'Bring up this people'; but thou hast not let me know whom thou wilt send with me. Yet thou hast said, 'I know you by name, and you have also found favor in my sight.' Now therefore, I pray thee, if I have found favor in thy sight, show me now thy ways, that I may know thee and find favor in thy sight. Consider too that this nation is thy people." And he said, "My presence will go with you, and I will give you rest." And he said to him, "If thy presence will not go with me, do not carry us up from here. For how shall it be known that I have found favor in thy sight, I and thy people? Is it not in thy going with us, so that we are distinct, I and thy people, from all other people that are upon the face of the earth?"

And the LORD said to Moses, "This very thing that you have spoken I will do; for you have found favor in my sight, and I know you by name." Moses said, "I pray thee, show me thy glory." And he said, "I will make all my goodness pass before you, and will proclaim before you my name 'The LORD'; and I will be gracious to whom I will be gracious, and will show mercy on whom I will show mercy. But," he said, "you cannot see my face; for man shall not see me and live." And the LORD said, "Behold, there is a place by me where you shall stand upon the rock; and while my glory passes by I will put you in a cleft of the rock, and I will cover you with my hand until I have passed by; then I will take away my hand, and you shall see my back; but my face shall not be seen."

MOSES:

SHINING FACES

IT WAS A FEARFUL AND BLOODY DAY, never to be forgotten in the history of Israel. We, with our modern laissez-faire approach to religion and morality, find the incidents barbarous, unacceptable. We feel sickened by the atrocity of sword-carrying Levites slashing their way through cowering ranks of guilty Israelites and killing three thousand of them in an orgy of retribution.

Our values have changed. To Moses the bloodshed was not to be compared with the horror of the people's sin. Having been delivered from Egypt by a God who changed the course of nature, who opened up the Red Sea, who led them himself by a pillar of cloud and fire, a God who revealed himself as the only God, the eternal God, the true God—the shallow Israelites had in a few petulant days dismissed him from their minds and had fallen back into idolatry. Their fickleness and their blasphemy appalled Moses; his horror was even greater because he had arrived among them after being in the immediate presence of the same God whose name they had so lightly defiled.

Two Loves

About one thing we may be clear. Moses may have been outraged, but he still deeply loved the very people on whom he turned the Levites' swords. He was a man torn between what seemed to be two incompatible loves: a love for God and a love for his people.

Several hours before, shrouded in mists and smoke, he had pleaded with God for the very people among whom God had dealt death. "Now therefore let me alone, that my wrath may burn hot against them and I may consume them," he heard God saying, "but of you I will make a great nation."

Was God testing him? Moses' response was immediate and unequivocal. Determining in his mind to give his life if need be in the struggle he "set himself to placate the LORD his God" (Ex. 32:11 NEB).

The temptation of God's offer, when you stop to think about it, could have been irresistible. The Israelites had been a source of endless tension and worry to Moses. He had been the first to put up with their fickleness, their querulousness, to feel the smart of their ingratitude, to be burdened with their endless wranglings. They had cheered him when he triumphed, but had ever been ready to turn on him when the least obstacle arose. What a relief it could have been to be rid of the whole undisciplined mob and to begin again with himself and his own children. But the thought never seems to have penetrated his mind. Two things dominate his prayer: his tender concern for the nation he led and his passionate jealousy for the reputation of his God.

"O LORD, why does thy wrath burn hot against thy people, whom thou hast brought forth out of the land of Egypt with great power and with a mighty hand?" Can this be the same Moses who had so strongly resisted God's call at the burning bush? The same prince of Egypt who had buried himself in the desert for forty years to get away from the dangers and heartaches of his people? Is it the same Moses who so recently had ordered the slaughter of three thousand Israelites? What has happened to him? Why is he so desperate that God's favor should rest upon two million fickle men and women in their Dionysian revels at the foot of Mount Sinai? And for whom is he more concerned, for the people or for the name of God?

"Why should the Egyptians say, 'With evil intent did he bring them forth, to slay them in the mountains, and to consume them from the face of the earth?'" It matters little which concern was greater. Moses the meek, Moses the timid is now transformed into a man who dares to challenge the wishes of God and even to upbraid him. Had the mountain changed him? Was there something intoxicating about Sinai where God was present as fire and smoke that made Moses lose his senses?

"Turn from thy fierce wrath," Moses beseeches, "and repent of this evil against thy people." Bold words indeed. It is the boldness of a bear at bay with her whelps, of a lioness whose kittens are threatened. He is oblivious to personal danger. One thing matters to him: that Israel be delivered from the consuming fire. This is the Moses we must see when we think about the slaughter in the camp.

Have you ever prayed like that? Have I? Are we in fact supposed to? Clearly we cannot work ourselves up artificially to the pitch of feeling that impelled Moses along his perilous course. Yet why is it that we go our ways unconcerned by the judgments of God that threaten his people today, smiling our evangelical smiles and praying, "God bless our church. Amen"?

Is it that we have never visited Sinai? Never seen the burning holiness of the God whose laws express the consuming fire of his being? Have we become so drenched with the spirit of the age we live in that sin has become a theological technicality? Does the prospect of divine wrath and judgment strike us as remote? Inconceivable? Do we, worse still, see pleading for God's mercy as being incompatible with the once-for-all sacrifice of the Lamb of God?

Our God remains a God of holy judgment. When the Lord of the churches dictated his letter to Thyatira he spoke of "the woman Jezebel, who calls herself a prophetess and is teaching and beguiling my servants to practice immorality.... I gave her time to repent, but she refuses to repent of her immorality. Behold, I will throw her on a sickbed, and those who commit adultery with her I will throw into great tribulation, ... and I will strike her children dead" (Rev. 2:20-23). It is John the beloved who takes down the dictation, and Jesus the meek and lowly who dictates the fiery threats. What reason have we to suppose that he has changed over the last two thousand years?

The God of Sinai is the God of our Lord Jesus Christ. He is immutable. He does not mellow with the passage of time. He is the God of law. He is the God of grace. He is the God who demands nothing less than holiness of his people. His self-appointed public relations experts have done us and him a blasphemous disservice in toning down the harsh outlines of his image, making him more suitable to our preference in gods. His image has changed with the times. We are worshipers of a golden calf. We need to be reminded, as were the subjects of C. S. Lewis's Narnia tales, that "Aslan is not a tame lion." We cannot pray right if we fail to recognize these things.

If you are to know the boldness and passion of Moses' prayer you must stand where Moses stood. You must see our God as a consuming fire. You must stand in his presence and listen to the uncompromising clarity of his judgments and laws. Read again the books of Exodus and Leviticus. Read them prayerfully and with an open heart. They are, though you may have forgotten it, still part of Holy Writ. Do not be afraid to let their standards grip you. Kneel down in awe be-

fore the pillar of fire. Your vision has been distorted. Your
values are corrupt. Only as you let his Word sink deep into
your will, will you see sin for the horror that it is. Only then
will you know that no step is too drastic to deal with it, be it a
Calvary or a casting into a bed of pain. Golgotha only makes
sense in the light of Sinai. You can never experience the urgency of intercession until you see sin from God's perspective.

Moses continues to plead. He has urged upon God the
honor of his own name ("Why should the Egyptians say, 'With
evil intent did he bring them forth, to slay them in the mountains . . .'?"). Moses also reminds him, as every intercessor
does, of God's own promises and covenants. "Remember
Abraham, Isaac, and Israel, thy servants, to whom thou didst
swear by thine own self. . . ."

There is a subtle emphasis in Moses' plea. He could have
spoken of God's servants Abram, Isaac and Jacob. Instead he
uses their covenant names, Abraham, Isaac and Israel. In doing so Moses makes clear to God how seriously he takes God's
dealings with his servants in the past. And this too carries a
lesson for us. For the God with whom we are called to plead is
the God of Moses, the God of David, the God of Elijah, Elisha
and Paul. If he does not change, then he can deal with us as
he dealt with them, delighting to make his arm as bare now as
in days gone by. Our faith rests upon the unchanging character of God as revealed by his acts in human history. And the
heart of God is gladdened as he listens to Moses. He has found
yet another man who refuses to accept him as less than the
God who revealed himself in history.

Reflecting God's Heart

Yet Moses is not satisfied. Has God accepted his plea? As the
burial of the dead proceeds he sets out again to climb into the
cloud-covered mountain. "Perhaps I can make atonement for
your sin," are his last strange words to the Israelites.

The prayer that follows is beautiful and moving. He freely

admits the horrendous sin of his people. "Alas, this people have sinned a great sin; they have made for themselves gods of gold." There are no excuses for sin. It is true that temptation under some circumstances is harder to resist than under others. It might also be true that extenuating circumstances can from our point of view mitigate the offense. But sin is sin. To say "It's in my family" is irrelevant. Cancer is not less deadly because we have some explanation for it. Nor is sin.

And as we look at the church around us we must adopt the same outlook. Sin is always sinful. It is always abhorrent. Mercy we may plead but not on the ground of extenuating circumstances. God is aware of extenuating circumstances, but the terrible nature of sin remains unchanged.

Yet Moses' prayer is not one of criticism or condemnation. He is simply laying the cards on the table. He is desperate. He is too keenly aware of God's all-seeing eyes to do anything less. He also is aware that God has the right to do whatever he pleases, yet pleads, "But now, if thou wilt forgive their sin." If we are to pray as he did, we must be aware of the same things and have that same attitude. We do not condemn but we dare not close our eyes.

Then comes the acid proof of a true intercessor. "And if not, blot me, I pray thee, out of the book which thou hast written." Moses will stand or fall with his people. Not for him the new start of a new nation. He could probably give no explanation for his feelings. But the end of Israel would be the end of everything for Moses.

His prayer is not melodramatic. On his way up the mountain he had time to reflect on God's earlier suggestion, and his mind is made up. God may do as he wishes. But Moses' destiny is bound up with the people he led out of Egypt. They may be fickle. They may be sinful. But they have become Moses' people just as much as they are God's people. He will live to lead them or die with them in the desert.

It would be good if more Christians viewed churches in

the same way. We may with no thought of criticism admit to God and to ourselves that we deserve, in our blatant greed and materialism, no mercy from a just God. Everything depends on the stance we choose to take. Is the church "they" or is it "we"? Are we concerned enough to stand with them should God's judgment fall? Do we love them in spite of what we see? Are they still God's people and ours?

"For I could wish that I myself were accursed and cut off from Christ for the sake of my brethren, my kinsmen by race," writes Paul (Rom. 9:3). Again, it is the stance of the true intercessor. Far from being a human attempt to defy God in his judgments, it is a reflection of God's very heart. He who died for the sins of mankind made that much clear to us all.

If prayed sincerely, it is a prayer that delights God. Yet it is a prayer that he never answers. God's response to Moses makes this clear. "Whoever has sinned against me, him will I blot out of my book" (Ex. 32:33).

The matter is still not ended, however. The danger of living in God's immediate presence has to be brought home to Israel. They are to proceed to Canaan. "But I will not go up among you, lest I consume you in the way, for you are a stiff-necked people," they were told (Ex. 33:3). They were instructed to strip themselves of their ornaments as a sign of mourning. Moses himself pitched a tent some distance from the main encampment (the tabernacle was not yet constructed) calling it the Tent of the Presence. A solemn ritual developed. All the nation would stand as Moses walked out toward it and would watch as the pillar of cloud descended over the tent the moment Moses entered it (Ex. 33:10). God was no longer in the midst of his people. As the cloud descended, all Israel would fall face down into the dust.

For Moses it was a privilege and a glory. "Thus the LORD used to speak to Moses face to face, as a man speaks to his friend" (Ex. 33:11). Yet he was not satisfied. For many of us it would be more than enough. If we could share the immediacy

43

and intimacy that Moses enjoyed, what would it matter to us that others lacked it? Yet to Moses this was all-important. He wanted not only mercy for God's people, but God's very presence among them. If I may paraphrase his words, "It is all very well to tell me you love me, that you know me, that I enjoy your favors. Well, if all this is true, teach me your ways so you won't leave us. Give us the chance of learning to please you. There is no point in our proceeding to Canaan without you. What difference will there be between us and any other nation if your presence is no longer among us? How will anyone know that we enjoy your favor?" (Ex. 33:12-16).

If only people would so plead for the church! For God is not in our midst. We worship the golden calves of material prosperity, of worldly prestige and respectability, of academic degrees and political power. Our successes are less the product of the Holy Spirit than of our technical proficiencies. The world can easily understand how well we do. We have the machinery and we know how to use it. No supernatural explanation of our expansion is needed. Who needs God? He is our figurehead, our logo. His photograph has the place of honor in our corporation board rooms. But he is chairman emeritus; and we, unlike Israel, do not even miss him.

God responded to Moses' prayer. He responded to it because he had himself taught Moses to pray as he did. God answered the prayer he had longed to hear. His presence would indeed accompany them.

Reflecting God's Glory

But still Moses was not satisfied. Suddenly he was seized by a longing that forced strange words from his mouth. You see his love for God's people was not really at variance with his love for God's person. The two loves were not distinct but one. With trembling daring he takes a further step into the thick darkness that shrouds God's brilliance. "Show me thy glory" (Ex. 33:18).

It is no longer for Israel he pleads. He can no more explain his new request than he could the attitude that drove him to make his first. He is caught by gales of the Spirit and he cannot avoid requesting to see God's glory any more than he can control his physical appetites. He is like a man who has come too close to a woman and finds himself with shaking hands incapable of self-control. He yearns for God with a passion that demands to be expressed. *"I pray thee, show me thy glory."*

Have you been there too? Once again it is not a matter of prodding yourself into a feeling state. Feelings follow faith. It is as if by faith we draw near to the God of the Scriptures that he one day may so disclose himself to us, that the passion that shook Moses will shake us too. Meanwhile we are not to be interested in passion but by faith to focus on Christ.

God granted Moses' final request, at least insofar as it was possible. From a crack in the rock Moses caught a glimpse of God's back. What image do the words conjure up in your mind? What is God's glory? The shining of brilliant light and color? Does it have to do with size and magnificence? Is God merely big?

If you have seen that glory, even the glory of his back, words will be pale and sorry things to tell about it. How can I describe, for instance, what an immediate vision of God's compassion looks like? It looks somewhat like dark and powerful seas rolling in thunderous power. But what have I said? My words convey no glory. They are powerless to bring you to your knees weeping uncontrollable tears at the sound of them.

Yet something did get through to the Israelites, a something more powerful than words. When eventually Moses came back to the waiting Israelites, "Moses did not know that the skin of his face shone because he had been talking with God" (Ex. 34:29). Indeed his face continued to shine. The luminescence was renewed whenever he went into the presence of God, so he had to cover his face that the Israelites might approach him. He who has seen God's glory reflects it.

To you it may seem that Moses' prayer experiences are beyond the likes of ordinary you. Let no one deceive you. Moses was weak and fearful. He led Israel, not because he chose, but because God called him.

God calls you too. You may or may not be destined to play a leading role in the fate of nations. But he wants to speak with you face to face, as a man speaks with a friend. He wants to share *his* concerns with you. He wants you to hold him to his own Word, something you can only do if you believe that Word. Read it with an open mind. Ask yourself, "Is there a God like this? What is his judgment on churches of today? Do I want to be his friend?" There is no impediment on his side. And the twentieth-century church could do with a few men and women with shining skin on their faces.

4

To the choirmaster. A Psalm of David, when Nathan the prophet came to him, after he had gone in to Bathsheba.

Psalm 51

Have mercy on me, O God,
   according to thy steadfast love;
   according to thy abundant mercy
      blot out my transgressions.
Wash me thoroughly from my iniquity,
   and cleanse me from my sin!

For I know my transgressions,
   and my sin is ever before me.
Against thee, thee only, have I sinned,
   and done that which is evil in thy sight,
so that thou art justified in thy sentence
   and blameless in thy judgment.
Behold, I was brought forth in iniquity,
   and in sin did my mother conceive me.

Behold, thou desirest truth in the inward being;
   therefore teach me wisdom in my secret heart.
Purge me with hyssop, and I shall be clean;
   wash me, and I shall be whiter than snow.
Fill me with joy and gladness;
   let the bones which thou hast broken rejoice.
Hide thy face from my sins,
   and blot out all my iniquities.

Create in me a clean heart, O God,
   and put a new and right spirit within me.

Cast me not away from thy presence,
    and take not thy holy Spirit from me.
Restore to me the joy of thy salvation,
    and uphold me with a willing spirit.

Then I will teach transgressors thy ways,
    and sinners will return to thee.
Deliver me from bloodguiltiness, O God,
    thou God of my salvation,
    and my tongue will sing aloud of thy deliverance.

O Lord, open thou my lips,
    and my mouth shall show forth thy praise.
For thou hast no delight in sacrifice;
    were I to give a burnt offering, thou wouldst not be
    pleased.
The sacrifice acceptable to God is a broken spirit;
    a broken and contrite heart, O God, thou wilt not
    despise.

Do good to Zion in thy good pleasure;
    rebuild the walls of Jerusalem,
then wilt thou delight in right sacrifices,
    in burnt offerings and whole burnt offerings;
    then bulls will be offered on thy altar.

DAVID:
FELLOWSHIP RESTORED

DAVID'S AFFAIR WITH BATHSHEBA shows a treacherous side to his nature. Power had corrupted him.

His decision to entrust war to his generals may have been a matter of laziness. His idle wandering on the rooftop after an afternoon nap during a time of war is inconsistent with his responsibilities. His voyeurism and lust for Bathsheba show his weakness as a man and his abuse of prerogatives as a king. He saw her, he lusted after her and he ordered her to come to the palace. You will find the whole story in 2 Samuel 11:1—12:25.

Perhaps Bathsheba is not without blame. Did she realize she could be observed as she bathed in the garden? Did she perhaps wish to be observed? We do not know. If she were innocent of exhibitionism, the invitation to the royal bed would put her in an awkward position. Yet it takes two to commit adultery, royal or otherwise, and Bathsheba showed no resistance.

People in Prayer

According to God's law for Israel David had already committed two sins, one of which carried a death sentence. He had simultaneously lain with a woman during her "impurity," and committed adultery. The king should be the first to keep the law, but the king had broken it. Had he been leading his army, the incident would never have occurred.

The lesson for us is plain. If we are doing *what* we should be *when* we should be, we shall be less exposed to temptation. Obedience to God carries protection with it. David had lost that protection and he succumbed to temptation.

A Leader without Excuse

Had matters ended there it would have been bad enough, but what follows is sordid and shameful. Bathsheba sent word to David that she was pregnant. David instantly recalled her husband from the battlefield, obviously hoping that he would have sexual relations with Bathsheba and not suspect subsequently that her child was sired by someone else.

But matters did not work out as David had hoped. David politely inquired of Uriah how the war was progressing, then excused him so that Uriah could visit his wife. But Uriah, stating that he could not enjoy domestic felicity while his fellow Israelites endured the hardships of a battlefield, refused to go home. His refusal included a significant detail. The ark of the Lord was with the Israelite army. Uriah felt that his place was by the ark and not in bed with his wife. Suavely David suggested he remain another day in Jerusalem.

The next night David got Uriah drunk and sent him on his way, hoping that wine would do what David's diplomacy had failed to. But Uriah was not drunk enough to change his convictions. He slept in the palace in the servants' quarters.

Then came the most sinister turn in the course of events. David made a decision which had far-reaching consequences in his own family life and in his relations with Joab, the commander-in-chief of his army. It is impossible to exaggerate how widespread the consequences were. He wrote a letter to Joab suggesting that Uriah be exposed to maximum danger on the battlefield, clearly hinting to Joab that he wanted the man killed. The rest of the story is history. Uriah died. Joab, knowing David's secrets, gained a measure of ascendancy over him, of which he made full use subsequently. Bathsheba was transferred to the palace to be comforted by David.

Yet David was not allowed to retain his guilty complacency. In a dramatic confrontation with the prophet Nathan, his sins were denounced. It is at this point that David's better qualities became apparent.

I too have been in the unhappy business of confronting leaders with their sins. Their reactions vary. To many the big questions are, "Who told you? (The dirty rat!)" "Who else knows about it?" Or "O.K., well, O.K. I *did* do it. Mind you, I think you've got a distorted picture of the whole thing. I don't know why she twists the story and exaggerates so much." Common to such responses are a preoccupation with the sinner's public image and an attempt to make excuses for the sin.

In David's case neither reaction occurs. In the face of Nathan's charges he makes one simple statement, "I have sinned against the LORD" (2 Sam. 12:13). No excuse is recorded. David makes no attempt to play down his sin.

Let us pause a moment. Sin is common to us all. We may be scarcely conscious of some sin. But God lays his finger on other sins. We grow troubled and confused, wondering how to deal with them.

If a guilt problem has you in its grip, turn to Psalm 51. No other chapter in Scripture presents so lucid a model of how a man should come to grips with it.

And we need a model, for questions bewilder us. Am I truly repentant? Will God hear me? Is the gravity of my sin such that it calls for special treatment? Why did I have to do it in the first place?

51

People in Prayer

The beauty of the example I have chosen lies precisely here. We are dealing in Psalm 51 with a horrendous crime committed by a man of God. You who read these lines may have committed adultery, but it is unlikely that you have murdered your lover's spouse. Whatever your sin may be, it will probably be no worse than David's. You may feel, however, that someone "in my position" or "with my responsibilities" ought not to commit the sin you are guilty of. (David was God's anointed king.) You feel it is all the worse because you ought to have known better. You have witnessed to others; you have taught others. (So had David.) If some people knew what you have done, . . .

If other people knew? Perhaps another problem lies here. You are unable to look squarely at your sin because your self-esteem gets in the way. Your dejection arises partly from humiliation. Your feelings of guilt are mingled with shame.

You cannot deal with sin until you look it in the eye. Undress it. Strip off the jacket of excuses you made to cover its ugliness. Tear away shirt, pants, everything that hides its nakedness, then say, "This is my child. I, and I alone am responsible for it." Look in your mirror too. The person staring back at you is quite capable of committing the same sin tomorrow. The person staring at you has sinned. Tell that person so. Don't pull any punches. Say kindly but firmly that this is the sort of thing that person is all too capable of, and until he wakes up to that fact, progress in godliness is impossible.

I have sinned against the Lord forms the core of Psalm 51. This is David's prayer of contrition for incidents I have been describing.

Natural Consequences

It is not clear why David did not face the death sentence. Had the enforcement of laws concerning adultery lapsed? Nathan is obviously aware of them, for he says, "You shall not die" (2 Sam. 12:13).

Why does David not face death? It is not altogether clear. Commentators suggest that his repentance obtained divine mercy. The New English Bible, however, puts intriguing words into Nathan's mouth. "The LORD has laid on another the consequences of your sin" (2 Sam. 12:13). Do the words refer to the child that was to be born? To the coming Lamb of God? Who was to suffer for David's sin? Again we cannot be sure.

At any rate David is to be pardoned. His prayer of contrition is heard, but the natural consequences of his action follow his career with fearful inevitability.

Yes, he was to be pardoned. And so are you. But as in David's case there may be natural consequences of your sin as well as the spiritual consequence of alienation from God. The alienation can be dealt with. The natural consequences may be a different matter.

One of my boys was involved with other youths in smashing up a car. Subsequently, because of his conversion, he besought God's forgiveness for his sin and knew what it meant to have peace with God. Yet he still had to face a judge in the juvenile court. He was still told to pay his share of the damages to the car—a cost that the judge wisely suggested be paid out of his own earnings.

David as well had to face natural consequences of his sin. For instance, the pregnancy did not disappear once David was forgiven. Nor did Joab, as I have already mentioned, forget that he had a hold over David.

Yet here again we begin to see why David is a man "after God's own heart." It is not the social and political consequences of his sin which form David's prime concern. His yearning is for fellowship with God. This above all else he pleads for. Other relationships may be damaged or destroyed, but his relationship to Jehovah must remain intact. "Have mercy on me, O God, according to thy steadfast love; according to thy abundant mercy blot out my transgressions. Wash me thoroughly, . . . cleanse me. . . ."

53

People in Prayer

I referred earlier to the excuses people make for their sins. If you have sinned, you have sinned. The basis of God's forgiveness to you is never that "you could hardly be blamed under the circumstances." Extenuating circumstances do not constitute a basis for mercy. Your only hope for mercy is the character of God. "Have mercy on me, O God, according to thy steadfast love; according to thy abundant mercy...." Your sins may be as miserable or as horrendous as David's. In either case hope is in God alone. He can pardon and cleanse because of who he is ("a righteous God and a Savior," Is. 45:21) not because you deserve another chance. You do not. None of us does.

I stress the point because to the degree that we attempt to excuse ourselves, to that degree we are not trusting the righteousness of our Savior. We are saying that we deserve special consideration, whereas in fact we deserve nothing but death. We may be cleansed only because our sins were laid upon another.

We have a choice to make when we come to God about our sin. Either we justify ourselves, or else we justify God. We cannot do both. If I am right, then God is wrong. If I say, "You would be wrong to condemn me altogether because I cannot really be held responsible" and so forth, I am challenging the righteous judgments of God. Whether I realize it or not, I am putting God in the wrong. (Moreover I am not asking God to forgive me but to excuse me, which is a very different matter.) But to admit my full responsibility is also to admit that God is right.

David chose to justify God rather than himself. "For I know my transgressions.... So that thou art justified in thy sentence." True confession consists of agreeing with God's assessment of my actions.

Two-Dimensional Justice
Nathan's technique as he confronted David with his sin was

masterly in its dramatic effect. He told David a story about a poor man whose sole capital and only comfort was a ewe who slept in his bosom every night. One day a rich man seized the ewe to kill and feed it to his guests. As he told the tale Nathan skillfully played on David's feelings of outrage. In the denunciation that follows we might have expected Nathan to reproach David bitterly with wrongs he did against Uriah and Bathsheba. Both wrongs are mentioned, but the emphasis lies elsewhere. "Why have you despised the word of the LORD, to do what is evil in his sight?" (2 Sam. 12:9). "You have despised [God]. . . . By this deed you have utterly scorned the LORD. . . ." (2 Sam. 12:10, 14).

We tend to see the social context of sin rather than its divine context. Human relationships are more important to us than relationships with God. Consequently it shocks us when David states in his confession, "Against thee, thee only, have I sinned, and done that which is evil in thy sight." We ask in protest, "Against God only? What about his sin against Uriah?"

But we fail to see the point. God is the God of the poor and the defenseless. He is the God of the man whose sole possession was a ewe lamb. He is the God of Uriah and of Bathsheba. In wronging them David has done something yet more outrageous, he has scorned and despised the one who declares himself to be their God. To murder Uriah was to commit a blasphemous crime against Uriah's God. Murder itself, terrible though it may be, is as nothing in the face of David's defiance of his Maker.

Nathan knew it. David knew it. But we, so absorbed with our two-dimensional concepts of justice, fail to see why sin against our neighbor is so wrong. Our God is too small and our concepts of sin too innocuous. God is not to be used as the rubber stamp for what we approve or disapprove, for he is the holy and mighty defender of the wronged, the despised and the weak. Social sin is sin directed against his very person.

People in Prayer

Murder was something David's conscience could accommodate. But to murder a man who belonged to God made a profound difference. Lady Macbeth had only the ghost of Duncan to contend with. David found himself face to face with an angry God.

His sin is larger than murder and adultery, as our own society conceives of them. It constitutes defiance of the Most High and a breaking of his laws.

Do you view your sins against others so? In hurting your brother do you see you are defying your brother's God? God has made himself responsible for your brother's well-being. (It is bad enough to kick the neighbor's dog, but woe betide you if the neighbor catches you doing it! He sees the offense as an affront to his person as well as an injury to his pet.)

Far from trying to minimize his wrong against Uriah, David is seeing it in a more serious light, and we would do well to do the same. God is your brother's keeper. He is the God of the girl or fellow you seduced, of the neighbor you snubbed, of the customer you shortchanged. You *wrong* your neighbor, but you *sin* against God.

Where the Blame Lies

David goes further. Not only does he admit his sin, making no excuse for it, recognizing its gravity and commending himself to the mercy of God alone, he also recognizes the corruption at the very core of his nature. He acknowledges that he has sinned against God and admits that he is hopelessly sinful: "Behold, I was brought forth in iniquity, and in sin did my mother conceive me."

He is not excusing himself. Rather, he is deploring the kind of person he is. He is in no position to say, "If you forgive me this time I won't do it again." He needs the mercy of God for what he *is* as well as for what he has done.

Your sinfulness is never an excuse for your sin. You have, it is true, a fallen nature. Like Paul, you groan that mortality

56

might be clothed with immortality. But wretched person that you are, sin overwhelms you. You do not know how you will ever overcome your weaknesses. It is important that you acknowledge this, not as an excuse, but as a recognition of your utter sinfulness.

The acknowledgment must not be one of self-pity. It will not do to say, "I'm no good anyway. I'm totally rotten and I never will be able to quit sinning." Don't be so petulant. You must not blame God, which is exactly what you do when you talk like this. You are bitter because you do not like what you see. And so long as you remain bitter and resentful, so long as you cannot accept yourself without resentment, you do not *confess* what you are to God; you only *complain* about it. Complaints never lead to healing. Confession does.

The behavioral sciences give us an apparent out. We are what we are, they tell us, because of what has happened in our past. We are the products of learning, of environment, of heredity or whatever. Therefore we may legitimately blame our parents, our siblings, society generally or even the Establishment for our defects. The doctrine of original sin, wrongly taught, may give us a similar out.

But the child of God accepts the responsibility for what he is. In saying he was conceived in sin, David is not blaming his parents. He is simply acknowledging a fact. The whole tone of his prayer indicates that he accepts all the responsibility.

This is hard for many of us. We prefer to find reasons for what we are, reasons that diminish our own responsibility. Yet whether it makes sense or not we are responsible for what we are as well as for what we do. And the tragedy is that until we accept our responsibility we cannot be helped.

You may say, "How can I be responsible for what I am when other people made me what I am?" Theologians differ in the kind of answers they supply to this question. Perhaps a simple illustration will help to make the idea more acceptable. Let us suppose that you inherit from your father a large estate but that there are many debts against the estate. You talk it over and think that with energy and with new ideas you can clear up the financial difficulties. But you fail. You fail partly because you are not as hardworking or skillful as you thought you were and partly because you began with certain odds against you.

Now you could say, "It's not my fault. If my father had not made such a mess of things I would not be in this position today." Yet you are in that position. Your excuse will not interest your creditors. It is irrelevant. To blame your father might help your bruised ego but it will not change things. You have no choice but to accept the responsibility of your debts. As a matter of fact, whether you are faced with bankruptcy or not, the only attitude which will allow you peace of mind, indeed the only mature attitude, will be, "I may as well face the fact that I'm in a hopeless position. Excuses won't help. I'll just have to face the music myself." In the same way face the fact of your sin squarely, let down your defenses, and then God can help you.

Changing the Leopard's Spots
It is here that the heavenly court has advantages over an earthly one. A prisoner charged with a criminal offense may be asked, "Are there any other offenses you would also like to be taken into account?" Certain advantages may follow his confessing previous violations of the law. But the law with its "correctional" institutions can do nothing for the prisoner who says, "I've had a criminal nature ever since I was born." We would all like to think it could, and there are probation officers, psychologists and psychiatrists all doing their best to change the leopard's spots. But the fact of the matter is that only God's miraculous grace can cleanse a defiled nature. And even divine grace is powerless until and unless we clearly see, freely accept and fully acknowledge that we are basically sinful.

David: Fellowship Restored

We could have no hope were it not for the fact that God wants to clean us inside. Just as an African violet fiend loves to nurture the delicate leaves and flowers, so God loves to set about the inner cleansing of his children.

"Behold, thou desirest truth in the inward being." It is his delight. He hovers over its progress and development with joyful enthusiasm. However deceitful and dark your heart may be, he has an enthusiasm to clean it up. He likes to do so gently, but he is not averse to using more violent measures if he has to. "Purge me with hyssop," David pleads, thinking of the hyssop used to sprinkle blood in symbolic cleansing. But for us the words have a deeper significance. Our hearts can be sprinkled clean from an evil conscience with the blood of Jesus (Heb. 9:13-14). For us it is enough that Christ died for us. Our confessed sins are purged, not by the thoroughness of our confession, but by God's total acceptance of our perfect Redeemer. So when we pray, "Create in me a clean heart, O God," we are not begging a reluctant God to perform a distasteful task but only yielding to the ardent yearnings of one who delights in making hearts clean—even yours.

Yet what does it mean to be cleansed inside? Does it mean that the sinful tendencies themselves will be dissolved? This would be wonderful, but let us beware of an easy view of sin and its solution. Sin is like baked-on grime that the overnight oven cleaners are so good at dissolving. Spray overnight, wipe off the next morning and behold a shiny new oven! In this sense God will cleanse you utterly from sin. The filth and the grime will be wiped away like a slough of foam, and you will be as clean as new. However, no oven cleaner prevents grime from building up again. God's cleansing does not insure freedom from sinful tendencies.

To switch metaphors, pus may be dissolved and a wound cleaned, but the wound remains; until it is healed it may become reinfected. Sin may recur through our spiritual infirmities, but always the first step is for the wound to be cleansed anew. With time, healing and new growth may take place. But do not leap ahead of God. We are dealing with sin, with infection, with pus. Cleansing, sometimes repeated cleansing, must precede healing and new growth. The one process is instantaneous. It paves the way for the second. But unfortunately it can only guarantee it as we continue to bring our pus-filled wounds to the heavenly physician.

Yet how many times will he cleanse my sin as I confess? Seven times? Nay, I tell you, till seventy times seven.

How complete will the cleansing be? "Hide thy face from my sins," David begs, "and blot out all my iniquities." And he will do just that. He will not see them. He will only see us in his Son. Our sins will be as if they never were.

With cleansing comes renewal of fellowship and joy. We were made for fellowship and without it our lives will be incomplete. We are like sun-loving flowers, palely wilting in the shade. "Fill me with joy and gladness; let the bones which thou hast broken rejoice. . . . Restore to me the joy of thy salvation."

The worst effect of sin is alienation, alienation from God, alienation from his people. It is this that crushes our spirits and bones. We find ourselves surrounded by crowds while the weight of our aloneness makes us drag our feet in weariness. God seems far away. His Spirit is grieved and silent. In Bunyan's tale, *Pilgrim's Progress,* sin formed the burden strapped to Christian's back as he floundered in the slough of Despond. Our bones feel crushed.

We can recognize this state of affairs. God hears the cry of the lonely heart, and hastens to restore it. "Cast me not away from thy presence, and take not thy holy Spirit from me." David knew how his sin had broken his communication with God. Since fellowship with God was the first priority of his life, David was "a man after God's own heart." Therefore it was not merely cleansing he wanted but cleansing as a gateway to restored fellowship. For with that fellowship would come life, vigor, joy.

The Acceptable Sacrifice

He has also perceived that the mere offering of sacrifice is not enough. He could have gone through the ritual of trespass offering or burnt offering, but a man who continued to excuse his sin or who felt that an animal sacrifice was enough to satisfy God, was a fool. "The sacrifice acceptable to God is a broken spirit; a broken and contrite heart, O God, thou wilt not despise." David knew nothing of the Lamb of God who was to take away the sin of the world. But he did see that outward religious observances were no substitute for a right attitude toward God and sin.

We ourselves forget this. We try to compensate for sin by our twentieth-century sacrifices. We atone by trying harder, by being extra kind to someone we have hurt, by praying longer and more frequently. Yet none of these things are acceptable to God. He wants a broken spirit, a contrite heart. He wants us simply to say, "There is nothing I can do to make up for what I have done. I have done something which you, and you alone can put right." Like Lady Macbeth we rub our stained hands crying, "Out, out damned spot!" when all that is needed is to show God the spot and say, "I cannot make it clean."

David knew too (for as he prayed, he remembered his previous dealings with God) the upsurge of singing in a conscience set free from guilt. He knew how spontaneous and real was the testimony of such a man. "Then I will teach transgressors thy ways, and sinners will return to thee. . . . and my tongue will sing aloud of thy deliverance."

I knew the gospel for years and preached it to the conversion of many before I really grasped what it meant in the words of Luther to "sin boldly, but to rejoice and believe in Christ more boldly." With the discovery came not only release from a crushing conscience, but also an increased spirit of praise and thanksgiving and an ease in sharing my joy with others.

People in Prayer

Only God can open our lips to sing to him. But he delights to do it. "O Lord, open thou my lips, and my mouth shall show forth thy praise." Ransomed prisoners shout for joy and sing. With the lightening of our burden, our spirits soar again and our lips are unsealed. Suddenly we become aware of the church around us, and we pray with new boldness for brethren. As David attests in the final verses, "Do good to Zion in thy good pleasure; rebuild the walls of Jerusalem, then wilt thou delight in right sacrifices."

When exactly did David write the psalm? Before his ill-fated child died or after? I think before. His pleading for the child's life through prayer and fasting (2 Sam. 12:16) may have been earnest, but the child's death found David not depressed but ready to face life joyfully in God. Many troubles awaited him, family problems and political problems of an order which would have embittered a lesser man. But David had discovered the secret of restored fellowship with God, and for that reason he is still looked upon as the greatest king ever to reign over Israel.

5

**Daniel
9:1-19**

In the first year of Darius the son of Ahasuerus, by birth a Mede, who became king over the realm of the Chaldeans–in the first year of his reign, I, Daniel, perceived in the books the number of years which, according to the word of the LORD to Jeremiah the prophet, must pass before the end of the desolations of Jerusalem, namely, seventy years.

Then I turned my face to the Lord God, seeking him by prayer and supplications with fasting and sackcloth and ashes. I prayed to the LORD my God and made confession, saying, "O Lord, the great and terrible God, who keepest covenant and steadfast love with those who love him and keep his commandments, we have sinned and done wrong and acted wickedly and rebelled, turning aside from thy commandments and ordinances; we have not listened to thy servants the prophets, who spoke in thy name to our kings, our princes, and our fathers, and to all the people of the land. To thee, O Lord, belongs righteousness, but to us confusion of face, as at this day, to the men of Judah, to the inhabitants of Jerusalem, and to all Israel, those that are near and those that are far away, in all the lands to which thou hast driven them, because of the treachery which they have committed against thee. To us, O Lord, belongs confusion of face, to our kings, to our princes, and to our fathers, because we have sinned against thee. To the Lord our God belong mercy and forgiveness; because we have rebelled against him, and have not obeyed the voice of the LORD our God by following his laws, which he set before us by his servants the prophets. All Israel has transgressed thy law and turned aside, refusing to obey thy voice. And the curse and oath which are written in the law of Moses the servant of God have been poured out upon us, because we have sinned against him. He has confirmed his words, which he spoke against us and against our rulers who ruled us, by bringing upon us a great calamity; for under the whole heaven there has not been done the like of what has been done against Jerusalem. As it is written in the law of Moses, all this calamity has come upon us, yet we have not entreated the favor of the LORD our God, turning from our iniquities and giving heed to thy truth. Therefore the LORD has kept ready the calamity and has brought it upon us; for the LORD our God is righteous in all the works which he has done, and we have not obeyed his voice. And now, O Lord our God, who didst bring thy people out of the land of Egypt with a mighty hand, and hast made thee a name, as at this day, we have sinned, we have done wickedly. O Lord, according to all thy righteous acts, let thy anger and thy wrath turn away from thy city Jerusalem, thy holy hill; because for our sins, and for the iniquities of our fathers, Jerusalem and thy people have become a byword among all who are round about us. Now therefore, O our God, hearken to the prayer of thy servant and to his supplications, and for thy own sake, O Lord, cause thy face to shine upon thy sanctuary, which is desolate. O my God, incline thy ear and hear; open thy eyes and behold our desolations, and the city which is called by thy name; for we do not present our supplications before thee on the ground of our righteousness, but on the ground of thy great mercy. O LORD, hear; O LORD, forgive; O LORD, give heed and act; delay not, for thy own sake, O my God, because thy city and thy people are called by thy name."

DANIEL:
THE MAN WHO WAS GREATLY BELOVED

WE HAVE SEEN THAT PRAYER is the response to God's initiative. So far we have dealt with prayers from the lips of men with whom God spoke directly. Abraham saw God face to face. Jacob was attacked. David was confronted by a prophet.

With Daniel God's initiative is less obvious. "I, Daniel, was reading the scriptures and reflecting . . ." (Dan. 9:2 NEB). As his mind was gripped by the written Word, the urge to pray was born.

Yet there is no essential difference between Abraham and Daniel at this point. "Shall I hide from Daniel what I am about to do?" we almost hear God saying (see Gen. 18:17). The medium of communication is different. To Abraham it was the spoken Word, to Daniel the written. But the same God spoke with the same purpose in mind: to call his servants to pray.

Were we given a choice we would doubtless opt for visions and voices. To our untutored imaginations they seem so much more satisfactory. Yet a moment's reflection should change our minds.

A vision never stays. It goes away. You are left wondering, Did it really happen to me? The same is even more true of a voice—God's or anyone else's. With the passage of time a man's confidence in his subjective experiences (hearing voices, seeing visions) diminishes. The saner the man is, the more the rule applies. It is the unstable, the paranoid, the insane person who clings to subjective rather than objective reality. And did not Jesus remind us that if we are not willing to heed Moses and the Prophets, even a visitation from the dead will leave us unmoved (Lk. 16:31)?

Like Daniel we are given the written Word and the quickening Spirit. While it is true that there are subjective aspects to reading the Scriptures, words themselves do not go away. Nor do their meanings change. They may at times (though by no means always) lack the specificity of spoken words. But far from being less tangible, they are more so.

Daniel needed no voice. He was gripped by the written promise of God. It wrapped itself round his thinking and refused to go away. It created inner tension for him. The facts he observed around him clashed with the words "in the books." The current political scene gave rise to no hope of the return of his people to their homeland. Yet the words were specific.

Between the Word and the World

No conflict would have arisen had Daniel taken Scripture lightly or lacked a concern for his people. And it may be that the lack of agonized appeals to God from the church of the twentieth century indicates our lack of inner conflict. The Word is the Word, and the newspapers are the newspapers and never the twain do meet—in our souls, that is.

Daniel's concern had a prophetic dimension, yet it is not to this dimension I refer. The judgment, the wrath and the mercy of the God of Scripture are to many of us "tales told by an idiot, full of sound and fury, signifying nothing" in the world we encounter every day. We would not express it so. But to all intents and purposes, this is how it is. How otherwise could we bear the intolerable tension between what is written and what actually is? Why, for instance, do we remain un-moved to read that God is not desirous "that any should perish, but that all should reach repentance" (2 Pet. 3:9), while millions around us drift heedless into doom? Sophistries about God's "permissive" will are beside the point. Daniel's prayer rose out of a tension between God's written truth and the world he saw around him. Most of us experience no such tension. The Word drifts over us as the world drifts by us.

The tension to which I refer can be focused on a specific circumstance. A command or a promise of Scripture may bear upon an immediate situation in your own life. You ought, according to Scripture, to be able to forgive Mary Jane. You may say, "I *can't* forgive her. I've tried, but my feelings don't go away." Yet the Scripture brands your conscience: "As the Lord has forgiven you, so you also must forgive" (Col. 3:13).

Where Scripture and your experience clash, do not run away from the tension. Let it become the energizer of earnest prayer. In the Christian life you need *more* tension, not less, if you are to do the will of God.

Tension is the bête noire of modern life. We are supposed to avoid it at all costs. We are given drugs and psychotherapy to reduce our tensions. We practice yoga, TM, take long walks, rearrange our schedules—all with a view to keeping our terrible adversary at bay. There are even "Christian" ways of going about the same thing.

I would not condemn all our efforts. Some tension is need-less and destructive. But tension in spiritual things can be creative and life-producing. As Daniel grappled with the ten-sion between God's Word and "reality" he made no attempt to ease his personal inner state. He did not turn to the Lord

67

as a form of psychotherapy. So far as he knew, his appeal to God might well have caused tension to increase. His approach was purposive. He clearly determined that "reality" of the world around must be made to conform with the reality of God's Word. He was, as it were, prepared to settle down to see the matter through to a conclusion, whatever the cost might prove. He would give himself to prayer, to supplications, even to fasting, until some resolution was reached. Sensing his own possible guilt and responsibility in the conflict between what was and what should have been, he donned sackcloth (a sign of mourning) and poured ashes over his head. Daniel was playing no religious game. He meant business. The tension in his soul was driving him to find a solution at any cost.

Expectation and Agitation

So far I have spoken only generally about the conflict between God's Word and the world Daniel lived in. On the surface it seems simply a matter of Jeremiah's prophecy that Jerusalem would remain desolate for seventy years. The seventy years were now accomplished. Nothing had happened.

Yet as we examine the prayer we see that the matter is a far more serious one to Daniel than the failure of a prophecy. It concerned the God behind the prophecy. The matter of seventy years was only part of a whole.

Let us suppose that someone you knew well and trusted absolutely, say a close friend, wrote to announce that he would arrive by air to spend a few days with you. Let us suppose Peter gave you his time of arrival and his flight number. If the plane were to arrive without your friend, you would be concerned. You would inquire at the desk of the airline. You might wait for the next flight or even for the next two or three flights. "Something *must* have happened," you would say. "It's just not like Peter to not show up." Your unresolved tension would drive you to make telephone calls, to leave a message at the airport and to take whatever steps you could both to find out what had happened and to make provision for every possible contingency.

On the other hand if Peter were hopelessly scatterbrained and unreliable, if he had repeatedly failed to turn up or had turned up a month after he originally planned, you could afford to be much more casual about the whole matter.

Jeremiah the prophet had repeatedly warned his people of the coming judgment long before they were dragged into captivity. Still more important, Jeremiah's prophecies were themselves part of a larger whole. From the time of Moses on, trumpet blasts of warning and of promise had been sounded by prophet after prophet. The promises and warnings reflected God's own character and his covenant with his people.

Daniel was not fixing on an isolated text. He had seen the whole sweep of Scripture. And behind it he saw where the heart of Scripture lay: in the revelation of God's character, and of his purposes and attitudes to his people. It is one thing to get a letter from a careless friend saying, "I'll drop by to see you next week." It is quite another to get a letter from the husband or wife you have known and loved for fifty years saying, "I'm coming home for certain Wednesday of next week."

In a sense the seventy years was neither here nor there, just as the Wednesday is neither here nor there should the beloved spouse fail to turn up. The crucial issues are: Who made the promise? How has he or she behaved in the past? What could have happened that someone I know so well, someone who has never let me down before, should do so now?

It is understandable then that Daniel never once mentions the seventy-year period in his intercession. As a matter of fact his prayer is preoccupied with promises of a very different kind, promises (or threats) of what God had always said he would do if his people were to persist in sin. Most of all, it is preoccupied with God himself.

And is this also not understandable? As Wednesday fades

into Thursday, what is it that fills the mind of the anxious housewife? "I just *know* something must have happened. Harry *always* calls. He would never let me go on like this without trying to get some word through." It is the known character of her husband which forms the basis of her agitation.

Notice Daniel's preoccupation with God's character: "O Lord, the great and terrible God." To Daniel, God was real and totally reliable. He was the God whose majesty filled the universe, the God who taught his own people respect by his mighty acts and his terrible judgments, the God "who keepest covenant and steadfast love with those who love him and keep his commandments."

Such is the God Daniel addresses. Such is the character of which he is vividly aware. Does God's character grip your imagination? Do you know him as the God who swallowed up the host of Egypt in the Red Sea? The God who deals with idolatry among his people with ruthless severity? The God whose covenants are inviolable and whose power has no end? The God who never breaks a promise?

"To thee, O Lord, belongs righteousness." For Daniel there was no inconsistency between the severity and the mercy of God. He comes before God with no hint of rebuke on his lips. Seventy years may have come and gone, but Daniel's God has a character against which no charge may be brought. Yearning, pleading intercession can flow only from the heart of the man or woman who has come to know God. And if you want to know God as Daniel knew him, you must spend time "in the books," meditating on their precepts as the Holy Spirit illumines the face of Christ before your eyes.

No We/They Dichotomy

Unfortunately Daniel's knowledge of God reminded him vividly of the sins of his people. In the face of God's repeated commands and warnings, his holy standard, and his incredible longsuffering, Israel's sin seems the more heinous. Daniel cringes as he thinks of it. He is shocked and dismayed. A flood of remorse pours from his lips. "We have sinned and done wrong and acted wickedly; . . . we have not listened. . . . To us [belongs] confusion of face, . . . treachery . . . committed against thee."

Yet pause a moment. What kind of confession is this? Who is the man from whose lips such terrible admissions flow? Is he not the Daniel whose purity and integrity stand out against black corruption in high places? Does he not have a public record of godliness in the face of opposition? What of his prayerfulness, of his sanctity? How then can such a man pray, "We have sinned?" If anyone has a right to say, "My people have sinned," and omit himself from the confession, surely Daniel is the man.

No such distinction occurs to him. The we/they dichotomy is alien to his thinking. He and his people are one. He mourns the sins of people long dead as though they were a part of him. "To thee, O Lord, belongs righteousness, but to us confusion of face."

Herein lies a secret for would-be intercessors. You must not pray, "Have mercy on them, O Lord," but, "Have mercy on *us*." You may object and say, "How can I identify myself with unbelievers? I am a Christian. Many for whom I pray are unsaved and living in sin." Yet you are just as much part of a fallen race as those for whom you pray. You share the nature of our common forefather Adam. You are not better than they, only more fortunate. If you would pray, you must sit where they sit, stand where they stand, and say with Daniel, "Lord, we are sinners, we rebel constantly, have mercy on *us*."

What hinders you from praying thus? Are you more deserving of God's grace than others? Were you chosen for your superior potential? Was the disease of sin in your members more benign, more open to cleansing? Have you ceased to be part of the human race since you became a Christian? Or, to refer to our text, are you morally superior to a Daniel? Pray alongside those for whom you intercede. Take them by the hand and say, "To us, O Lord, belongs confusion of face."

However, to do this involves more than a change in words. It calls for a change in perspective. It demands that we take seriously the doom that hangs over the heads of other people and that we acknowledge God's right to bring judgment upon them.

If you are anything like me, you will grow uncomfortable at this point. As I chat with and rub shoulders with non-Christians around me, I blot out completely the thought that a sword hangs over their heads. Were any of them right now to be looking over my shoulder, I would be embarrassed to have them read what I am writing. I would grow defensive were they to ask, "Surely you don't believe *in a God like that?*" The problem is that I do not share Daniel's or God's perspective on the men and women I meet every day. Only when I do so, do my prayers for them come alive.

God's perspective is one of judgment. We all deserve the wrath of God. Hell is too good for us. And that means hell is too good for the non-Christians who surround us. The wrath of the Lamb is too good for the Christians we feel critical of. Daniel sees it with absolute clarity. "Therefore the LORD has kept ready the calamity and has brought it upon us; for the LORD our God is righteous in all the works which he has done, and we have not obeyed his voice."

We do not think like Daniel. Somewhere deep in our minds is a feeling (which we may not dare to acknowledge, even to ourselves) that maybe God is a little bit harsh with the nicer kind of non-Christians. And to think about God's wrath toward a brother or sister in Christ is inconceivable.

Crippling Fears

I may be probing a sensitive spot but I must proceed. You say, "Yes, but have we any right to judge people? After all, aren't we supposed to love them?" You are missing the point.

Daniel: The Man Who Was Greatly Beloved

People are already under judgment. We find ourselves reluctant to admit that God is doing the right thing when he judges them. But, reluctant or not, we are facing an either/or in God's relationship with us. Either he is in the right or we are. To be honest, my own conflict has always arisen because I don't want to believe that God is who he is. Yet I am setting up my disinclination as a standard to assess the righteousness of God.

As for loving people, I cannot help but feel that our "loving" attitude to their sin is like some people's attitude to sickness or accidents. I remember one teen-age boy who fell off his bicycle and broke his arm. It was so broken it looked bent. He ran into his father's office for help only to be greeted with the words, "Take it away! Take it away! You know I can't bear to look at things like that!"

It is not a sign of love to avoid thinking about people's sickness. It is not loving to avoid visiting a dying person "because I wouldn't know what to say." It is not loving (though it may be legally prudent) to avoid helping someone involved in an accident "because that sort of thing makes me feel ill." Rather it is a sign that we are crippled by fears that prevent us from facing reality.

In the same way our fear of sin and judgment are no demonstration of love. An intercessor is above all a realist. You cannot intercede like Daniel unless you see things as they are, including a world and even a church under the sword of judgment.

My wife and I had been in Bolivia only three months when our first child, a boy, was born. I watched the birth take place. If you had asked me how I felt, I'm sure I would have said, "I'm feeling great, thank you." Yet as I look back I know that I was extremely frightened.

Scott was born with badly clubbed feet. As he was lifted from the delivery table my wife cried, "John, look at his feet. There's something wrong with his feet!" I looked at the red,

73

wet, squirming body but *saw nothing wrong*.

"His feet are fine, honey," I retorted.

"But his feet, honey, look at his feet!"

I looked, but I did not see. "It's O.K., dear, his feet are just fine."

Such was my anxious need to feel that all was well that I was blind to the distorted limbs. Incredible as it may seem (for I am a physician and was trained to inspect babies as they were born) I saw no grotesquely twisted limbs, only straight ones. I did not know it at the time, but my fears made me blind to the reality that my son was born a cripple. I could not see what was under my nose.

Were the full impact of the fate of people around us to break over our minds, we might be too overwhelmed to pray at all. Some of us are blind to their fate in the same way and for the same reasons that I was blind to my son's legs. We are emotionally incapable of seeing the judgment that awaits them. Either we deny its reality or else we shield ourselves from its full impact, acknowledging the fact, but isolating ourselves from its horror. No urgency grips us as we pray. How can it when we hide ourselves from the truth?

What can we do? We can start by acknowledging to ourselves and confessing to God that we are indeed afraid to face the truth. We can read those parts of his Word that deal with judgment and let the Holy Spirit make them come alive to us. If we are perplexed that God should judge at all, we need to bring our perplexity to him and let him reveal more of himself to our hearts. And then, like Abraham, like Moses and like Daniel we will begin to intercede.

The Opinion of Ants

When a man prays like Daniel we may ask the questions, What drives him to prayer? Where do the prayer-energy and the zeal come from? We could answer with a cliché and say that the Holy Spirit inspired him, and doubtless this would be true.

Daniel: The Man Who Was Greatly Beloved

However, the Holy Spirit is not mentioned in the passage, and the answer may be of little help to you in changing your own prayer life. Doubtless you have often sought the Spirit and yielded to him, yet your prayers have not been living and earnest. You need to inquire in what way the Spirit can impart a sense of urgency to you.

Already we have seen the tension which started the prayer going: the conflict between the God Daniel knew and the facts of life around him. But there is more to it than that. Tension can account for the prayer's beginning but it hardly accounts for its wind-up. Daniel has become bold. He insists. He demands. And though we have no way of knowing, it hardly seems likely that he was using a prayer technique or acting a part.

It would be perfectly possible for us to imitate Daniel's words or even the posture he adopts before God. "O LORD, hear; O LORD, forgive; O LORD, give heed and act; delay not. . . ." We could say the same words. We could strut boldly before God and demand that he act, or according to the latest fad, thank him that he *will* act. But to do either can be no more than silly posturing. We may be doing nothing more than convincing ourselves, acting a role, fretting upon a stage. God is not impressed by acting, good or bad.

But Daniel was not acting. He spoke out of his deep concern, a concern for the honor of God's name. Six times in the latter part of his prayer he makes reference to the name, the reputation and character of God: "and hast made thee a name" (v. 15), "according to all thy righteous acts" (v. 16), "for thy own sake" (v. 17), "on the ground of thy great mercy" (v. 18), "for thy own sake . . . because thy city and thy people are called by thy name" (v. 19). Clearly he feels that God's reputation is at stake, and he is jealous for God's honor. He wants God to be vindicated in everyone's eyes. He cannot bear the thought that people should think little of God or compare him with false deities.

People in Prayer

For two reasons his stance is important. First, his appeal will touch a sensitive spot with God; in addition Daniel's concern about God's honor seems, as I have already noted, to add impetuous boldness to his prayer.

To talk about God having a sensitive spot is perhaps both inaccurate and irreverent. God has no psychological weaknesses. However there are reasons important to God which will impel him to action. He is jealous of his name and honor.

When we think of jealousy we do so in human terms. Jealousy is something we tend to see as a weakness, especially jealousy about one's own personal prestige or reputation. Yet God is plainly represented to us in Scripture as one who is indeed concerned about his honor and reputation, so that in pleading as he does, Daniel will undoubtedly have God's attention.

Human jealousy, your jealousy and mine, springs from weakness. It is the reaction of someone who is uncertain of his personal worth. It is for this reason that we grow concerned about our own reputations.

When we talk about God's jealousy, however, we are not talking about the same thing. God is supreme. He is aware of his majesty, his awesome power, his perfect righteousness, his unfathomable wisdom. Yet he is neither vain nor insecure. He has no need to prove anything. Would you be worried about what opinion a group of ants entertained concerning you? Of course not. Nor does God *need* to be concerned about what men think of him. Yet he is concerned.

There might be a set of exceptional circumstances under which you would worry about what a group of ants thought of you. Let us suppose for a moment that you have the power to raise ants from their condition to one of higher life and greater felicity. In addition let us suppose that you loved the little wretches and that you needed their trust if you were to give them the gift of a higher life form. Under those circumstances (depending, of course, on how much you loved them) you might be very anxious to make them aware of your power and your love. For their own sakes you would be jealous about your reputation among them. The depth of your jealousy would be the measure of your love. It would be a noble jealousy arising not from your personal insecurity but out of your concern for the well-being of the ants who would not be helped unless they understood and trusted your ability to help them.

Now perhaps we are in a position to appreciate God's jealous concern about the honor of his name (his character) among men. Our trusting adoration adds nothing to him, but it does make it possible for us to be delivered from our misery. He wants us to know him because he loves us and cares for us in our sad condition. The one thing that constantly hinders his power is our own inadequate view of God. Tozer used to say that what a man thinks of God is the most important thing about him and will determine the whole course of his life. He also said that a church's view of God would likewise determine its spiritual life and power.

Beyond Self

It seems evident that Daniel knew an altogether larger God than his contemporaries. It is equally evident that he grasped the importance of God's name being established and his honor being upheld before Jew and heathen alike. For this reason he stresses repeatedly such expressions as, "for thy own sake," "because . . . thy people are called by thy name." And in doing so he is striving effectively with God.

Praying in this way does something for Daniel too. It carries him beyond himself. He is not concerned anymore with his personal problems, but with God's honor. To the degree that his thoughts are occupied with the name of his God, he is lifted to a higher plane of praying.

To be self-centered is not in itself bad. Babies are utterly concerned with themselves. That is to say they are only concerned with others to the extent that others amuse them, feed them and give way to their wishes. Self-centeredness occurs naturally and properly at certain stages in development. Maturity brings with it a capacity to look beyond yourself so someone else's well-being becomes even more important to you than your own.

Spiritual growth may follow a similar course to physical growth. At earlier stages the Christian is more concerned about himself, his experiences, what other people think about him and what God's Word does for him. With spiritual maturing comes an increasing concern for others, and for the honor and glory of God. To the degree that we mature spiritually, our prayers will become theocentric, that is, God-centered.

You must remember, however, that while maturation is subject to its own laws and seems to take place automatically, training is also part of maturing. There would be no point in my writing about Daniel's prayer if you simply had to wait until you "matured" before you could pray as he did. Babies are taught. The natural process of maturation is supplemented at every point by parental example and instruction. So they are taught to feed themselves, to walk, to talk, to dress themselves and so on.

There is no reason to prevent you from doing exactly what Daniel did and becoming actively concerned about the name, the honor and the reputation of God among people around you. The prayer is recorded to teach you. It is intended to alert you to the lack of God-centeredness in your prayers. It may never have occurred to you that God's honor and reputation are subjects you should be praying about. The truth is that they should form the very basis of your praying. The Holy Spirit waits to lead you in such praying and in the measure that you let him teach you, your praying will rise to a higher plane too.

Needless to say you will not be concerned that his honor be

revealed if you lack an awareness of how great and wonderful he is. We are back at Tozer's idea, that a man's concept of God is the most important fact about him.

I have never been made more aware of God's reality, power and glory than I have on my recent rereading of the Old Testament. I see it with new eyes. I ask myself, "Did these things really happen? Did the ten plagues come at the word of Moses? Did the Red Sea divide? Did the rock pour out water? Did Jordan's waters roll back? Did a trumpet blast bring down the walls of Jericho?"

When I read David's bold words to Goliath they came shockingly alive to me and I wonder whether I would have dared to count on the God of Israel as David the slender stripling did: "You come to me with a sword and with a spear and with a javelin; but I come to you in the name of the LORD of hosts, the God of the armies of Israel, whom you have defied. This day the LORD will deliver you into my hand, and I will strike you down, and cut off your head . . . that all the earth may know that there is a God in Israel, and that all this assembly may know that the LORD saves not with sword and spear; for the battle is the LORD's and he will give you into our hand" (1 Sam. 17:45-47).

Magnificent! I catch my breath with wonder. Do I have such a view of God? He has not changed since those days. If my God is the God of David what may I not expect him to do when the honor of his name is on the line?

Go back to the Old Testament. Read the historical portions as an adult. They are not only "Bible stories" to entertain children in Sunday school, but history for grownups who are expected to take their implications very seriously. It may be that as you read, you will begin to pray as Daniel prayed. It may be that like him, you will become a man (or a woman) who is greatly beloved.

6

**1 Samuel
1:1-18**

There was a certain man of Ramathaim-zophim, of the hill country of Ephraim, whose name was Elkanah the son of Jeroham, son of Elihu, son of Tohu, son of Zuph, an Ephraimite. He had two wives; the name of the one was Hannah, and the name of the other Peninnah. And Peninnah had children, but Hannah had no children.

Now this man used to go up year by year from his city to worship and to sacrifice to the LORD of hosts at Shiloh, where the two sons of Eli, Hophni and Phinehas, were priests of the LORD. On the day when Elkanah sacrificed, he would give portions to Peninnah his wife and to all her sons and daughters; and, although he loved Hannah, he would give Hannah only one portion, because the LORD had closed her womb. And her rival used to provoke her sorely, to irritate her, because the LORD had closed her womb. So it went on year by year; as often as she went up to the house of the LORD, she used to provoke her. Therefore Hannah wept and would not eat. And Elkanah, her husband, said to her, "Hannah, why do you weep? And why do you not eat? And why is your heart sad? Am I not more to you than ten sons?"

After they had eaten and drunk in Shiloh, Hannah rose. Now Eli the priest was sitting on the seat beside the doorpost of the temple of the LORD. She was deeply distressed and prayed to the LORD, and wept bitterly. And she vowed a vow and said, "O LORD of hosts, if thou wilt indeed look on the affliction of thy maidservant, and remember me, and not forget thy maid-

servant, but wilt give to thy maidservant a son, then I will give him to the LORD all the days of his life, and no razor shall touch his head."

As she continued praying before the LORD, Eli observed her mouth. Hannah was speaking in her heart; only her lips moved, and her voice was not heard; therefore Eli took her to be a drunken woman. And Eli said to her, "How long will you be drunken? Put away your wine from you." But Hannah answered, "No, my lord, I am a woman sorely troubled; I have drunk neither wine nor strong drink, but I have been pouring out my soul before the LORD. Do not regard your maidservant as a base woman, for all along I have been speaking out of my great anxiety and vexation." Then Eli answered, "Go in peace, and the God of Israel grant your petition which you have made to him." And she said, "Let your maidservant find favor in your eyes." Then the woman went her way and ate, and her countenance was no longer sad.

HANNAH:

WHISPERS IN
PLEASURE,
SHOUTS IN PAIN

IN THE PREVIOUS CHAPTER I spoke about prayer of a
higher order. Yet terms like *higher* and *lower* bother me when
used in relation to Christianity. They suggest degrees of ex-
cellence, advanced spiritual performance, a sort of black belt
in Christian karate. Naturally we are expected to make progress. God wants us to grow in maturity. The Holy Spirit
works in us so that as we collaborate with him we grow more
Christlike.

I do not want to suggest, however, that the prayer I have la-
beled *higher* (prayer primarily concerned with the honour of
God's name) is meant to decrease the importance of prayer
about your personal needs. Surely the whole point of a good
relationship is its reciprocity. At times I listen with interest
and sympathy to a friend's worries; at other times I am comforted to know he will listen to mine.

So it is with prayer. As you grow in maturity, God's will,
God's purposes, God's honor will increasingly concern you.

People in Prayer

But however mature you may become, you will never cease to have griefs and joys of your own. If prayer that concerns God's honor is to be called higher prayer, I must make it clear that you must never stop appealing to God about your sorrows and heartaches. Lower prayer, if we are to adopt such an expression, will be necessary as long as you live. "Have no anxiety about anything," Paul writes to the Philippian church, "but in everything by prayer and supplication with thanksgiving let your requests be made known to God" (Phil. 4:6).

If ever a man penetrated the mysteries of prayer, Daniel was that man. By whatever yardstick we measure prayer life, its passionate intensity, its boldness, its penetration into prophetic mysteries, his was an outstanding life of prayer. Fortunately the same Bible records prayers of a simpler order with no suggestion that they are less important. I have chosen to discuss Hannah's prayer after Daniel's to remind both myself and you that we shall never outgrow the need of childlike prayer for personal needs.

Beloved but Barren

Hannah's was a common problem in a society where men kept more than one wife. Although she enjoyed more of her husband's love than her rival Peninnah, Hannah was barren. The mockery and gibes of her fertile rival, who would be surrounded in the household with her brood of offspring, made her husband's love a source of pain and bitterness to Hannah.

Nothing hurt her more than the annual feast of tithes. Israelites had the custom of reserving one-tenth of their produce to offer to the Lord. Elkanah, who lived some distance from Shiloh (where the tithes were celebrated), would convert his grain and cattle into silver, and take the silver in the leather bag to Shiloh. There he would buy meat, flour, wine and strong drink to his heart's content. With others he would give his sacrifice to the priest to be placed on the altar. After this the rest of the tithe, having been offered to God, would be eaten in the presence of God with much rejoicing by the family who made the offering. It was God's portion, but God had invited them to feast with him.

But for Hannah there was no joy. As Elkanah distributed God's portion of meat to his family he would load Peninnah's platter with large quantities of meat to divide among her young children. The single portion that Hannah received was a painful reminder of her barrenness. Peninnah lost no opportunity to rub salt in her rival's wounds.

One year Hannah left her food untouched. Tears welled from her eyes as she stared at the meat. Her appetite had gone. Even Elkanah's tender assurances of love could not remove the load of depression that crushed her.

Purpose in Pain

Hannah's plight is touching. But its very ordinariness raises the question: Why should so trivial a matter need to be recorded? Why should it form the opening bars in the long symphony of Israel's greatness?

True, the matter was anything but trivial to Hannah. For Hannah life held no meaning so long as she remained barren. Perhaps we can say then that the story is important for this very reason. In the long story of kings, battles, sieges and the exploits of the great, it tells of a God who cares for the poor and the downtrodden, of a God to whom no hurt is too trivial to demand his care. God is indeed the God of the sparrows and the lilies. His response to Hannah's grief is characteristic. Certainly this forms the theme of Hannah's song of triumph in the following chapter (a song which is remarkably similar to Mary's Magnificat).

But there is more to the matter than this. Her prayer represents a turning point in Israel's history. It closed an age which at times bordered on anarchy, a period of shame and humiliation, relieved only by brief periods of liberty and prosperity. It opened the door to the age of Israel's greatness. The opening bars of the saga are not there by chance. They form an integral part of the whole composition.

Yet to understand why this is so, we must remind ourselves again of the basic nature of prayer: a response to God's initiative. Yet if ever it seems God responds to human initiative instead of vice versa, surely it is with Hannah's prayer. She was in pain. She prayed about her pain. God answered beyond all her expectations. Hannah took the initiative and God responded.

Is this really the way it was? Does Hannah's prayer represent an exception to the rule? Who caused her to be barren ("the LORD had closed her womb")? Who allowed her to be subject to ridicule—and why?

Hannah's child was to be an unusual figure in history. He was by sheer moral and spiritual power in one lifetime to cleanse idolatry from Israel, to exalt the only true God throughout the realm and to establish a monarchy.

Unusual circumstances were needed to produce such a man. Greatness was to be formed in a special mold. From early childhood Samuel was to be subject to the influences of worship, of Eli's moral guidance and of the voice of God. When in her desperation Hannah vowed that any child born to her would be given back to God, she little knew the consequences her vow would have. But God knew. He had allowed her to come to a pitch of desperation for this very reason. The fruit of her womb would be reared in the temple.

Could God be so heartless? Did he aggravate her pain to force her unwittingly into making so desperate a vow? Could he be so unfeeling?

It was C. S. Lewis who once said that God whispers to us in our pleasures but shouts to us in our pain. The same pain that produced a Samuel to transform Israel, produced a transformed Hannah. If we could have talked with her ten years after the birth of Samuel (long before Samuel became a national figure) we would have found that she had never ceased to sound the praises of the God who had "tormented" her. She would laugh at the pain. Laugh at it not only because God had answered her but because pain had driven her into the arms of God.

I never know how one measures pain, but my heart swells with joy, a joy too great to express in words, at the thought of the trials my wife and I have gone through. What I have gained through them in sheer treasure makes the suffering a trivial price to pay. I hate pain, but I would gladly undergo the same pain again to find more of the same treasure. I can almost (but not quite) laugh at the memory of the pain. I can certainly smile wonderingly at the harvest of joy I have reaped.

Hannah was not a pawn in God's historical chess game. God's purposes for Hannah might have involved pain. But his larger purpose for Israel was linked with a loving purpose for Hannah. He led her gently through suffering that he might enlarge her capacity for joy. Thus, it was God, not Hannah, who took the initiative. The silent cries of her desperation were the response to pressures he was placing on her.

Spiritual Surgery
Personal suffering is never meaningless for the child of God. You may not know why you suffer, and your suffering may seem to you too painful to bear. Under such circumstances you must always bring your suffering to him and ask him to take it away. You may go further than Hannah and praise him that you know he is trustworthy and concerned, however great the pain may be. You may know (because of Hannah's story) that God could have plans to do something through your pain that extends far beyond your own life and times. In addition he may give you through the pain an increased capacity to help others who suffer. He may change the course of history through your pain, but you may never discover its wider meaning.

People in Prayer

What you can always experience is a deepening relationship with him. For you may be sure that the pain has a purpose in your own life. It is divine surgery that, if you respond to it appropriately, will heal and correct defects in your Christian growth. But it is essential that you respond with trust in the mercy and goodness of God. No bitterness or rebellion must be permitted to cloud your vision of him even when he seems not to answer. Otherwise the pain designed to enrich and deepen your relationship with him might have the opposite effect as you allow yourself the luxuries of self-pity and doubt.

Hannah's pain, as we have seen, drove her to make a vow. Her vow looks suspiciously like a bargain with God. If only he would grant her a child, she would lend him to the Lord for the rest of his life. The question naturally arises: Is this standard procedure when you make a request from God?

Vows attached to prayers are relative rarities in the Bible. Hannah's prayer is almost unique in this respect. Yet there can be little doubt that the vow was divinely inspired. Its consequences for Israel's history are hard to exaggerate.

It would be foolish, however, to infer that you should enter into prayer with the idea of bargaining with God. You have nothing to bargain with. The real lesson is that you acknowledge that whatever God gives, you owe to him alone. This was all Hannah was really doing. Samuel belonged to God because God gave him to Hannah. In the same way his answers to your prayers do not represent prayer achievements. To pat yourself on the back or to boast about your prayer triumphs is offensive to God. Whatever he may give you in answer to your prayer he gives by sovereign grace. You must acknowledge the fact to yourself and others. God has been good to you. He has given beyond anything you deserved. You are forever in his debt.

Strangely enough you will enjoy God's gifts far more when you perceive this. God gave my family a beautiful home a little while back. It contains luxuries we do not need, and (I trust) we would be willing to give it up at any time his service makes it necessary. Now I have observed that my feeling about the house is subject to remarkable fluctuations. In those moments when I remember that our home is indeed a gift from a gracious God, I am flooded with peace, with joy, with thanksgiving. At other times when I begin to pride myself in its superior qualities or to compare it in my mind with my friends' homes, my joy evaporates. Indeed the house becomes a positive burden. There are so many hedges to trim, trees to care for and odd jobs to be done that suddenly it looks very ordinary, even undesirable. While vanity clouds my eyes and burdens my heart, gratitude clears my vision and lightens my load. "Every good endowment and every perfect gift is from above, coming down from the Father of lights" (Jas. 1:17). It is essential that we recognize what we owe him. Otherwise his gifts will bring us no joy. Samuel, I am sure, was a lifelong joy for Hannah.

Longing Shot Like an Arrow

I often wish I could have watched Hannah's mobile lips framing silent words of longing as hour succeeded hour. Eli evidently did watch. Probably he frowned in irritation, turned away and came back to observe her several times. In the end his irritation overcame his discretion.

"How long will you be drunken? Put away your wine from you."

But Hannah was drunken with yearning, not with wine. "No, my lord, I am a woman sorely troubled; I have drunk neither wine nor strong drink, but I have been pouring out my soul before the LORD. Do not regard your maidservant as a base woman, for all along I have been speaking out of my great anxiety and vexation."

"Sorely troubled . . . pouring out my soul before the LORD . . . speaking out of my great anxiety and vexation. . . ." We do not need to know all she said. Her agonies are distilled into these three moving phrases. She could have spoken audibly, sobbed uncontrollably, lain on her face and groaned, moaned and swayed her body—but the message that pierced the heavens would have been the same. Longing is always understood clearly by God.

The point to notice is that it was directed longing, shot like an arrow from a bow at the target. Many people wring their hands and weep, but their weeping echoes hollowly through an empty universe . . . or so it must seem to them. And so for all intents and purposes it might as well be. "For whoever would draw near to God must believe that he exists and that he rewards those who seek him" (Heb. 11:6). Agony must be expressed to a God who is *there*.

God hears all poured out agony, but he longs to be something more than a celestial pacifier. He wants people in their suffering to come to him. For he is himself the gift we really need. Children can be placated with candy only for so long. It is the loving parent they want. Therefore go to him in your sorrow. "Draw near to God and he will draw near to you" (Jas. 4:8).

As Christians we often make two mistakes. We moan fluently to people around us. This may be the lesser evil. Friends can be counted on to take a certain amount of moaning. But we are to bring our griefs to God, and it is here that we fail so lamentably. We come to him. That is to say we exercise faith. We believe he *is*, that he is *there*, so to speak. We also believe that he can hear us. But our fear of God and our reverence for him inhibit us. Can the God of the heavens really care about my little affairs? (Does a mother care about a three-year-old's scratched finger?)

I want to say nothing that will diminish your reverence for God. Evangelical Christians are far too ready to treat God as a heavenly buddy. We are blind to his glory and deaf to the voice that is the sound of many waters. If I knew how to make you tremble and quake in his presence I would. Indeed I pray the Holy Spirit may do just that for you.

But to tremble and to be struck dumb need not go together. Great as he is, he is also tender and gentle. And since he is aware of the subtlest nuance of pain in our hearts we need not hide it from him. We may even be angry or resentful toward him, but whether our resentment is justifiable or not, it is better expressed than hidden. Does it shock you, once you see him, to see how horrendous your thoughts really are? Do not disguise them but confess them. Also tell him of your hurts. Time is of no consequence. You may talk for hours since he dwells in eternity where time has no meaning. And know that when you pour out your heart to God like Hannah did, he will be listening intently, understanding profoundly.

Peace came to Hannah. Eli's words of comfort were God's way of telling her that he had heard. Weeks might pass before she became pregnant, but for her the issue was settled.

My own experience has varied. At times peace that transcends my understanding has followed such an outpouring of my heart. God knows and that is enough. God knows, and sometimes I know the request has been answered, however long it may be before the heavenly parcel comes in the mail.

But there are other times when it is harder for me to know that peace. No flood of assurance flows through my limbs and lifts me to my feet. I am asked, "Can you trust me?" "Yes, Lord," I will answer. "Then trust me and leave the matter with me. You know who I am." And with this I have to be satisfied.

But with Hannah all was well—well for the deepest of reasons that Someone had heard and understood. And to know one is understood is to experience revolutionary changes within oneself. During the hours Hannah had spent pouring her heart out to God, great changes had come about in her. She was no longer the same woman who had refused to eat her portion of meat. She walked back to her family. She ate a hearty meal. Her eyes had a new light in them and a secret smile played about her lips.

7

**Job
38:1-7;
40:1-5;
42:1-6**

Then the LORD answered Job out of the whirlwind:
"Who is this that darkens counsel by words without
    knowledge?
Gird up your loins like a man,
    I will question you, and you shall declare to me.

"Where were you when I laid the foundation of the
    earth?
    Tell me, if you have understanding.
Who determined its measurements—surely you know!
    Or who stretched the line upon it?
On what were its bases sunk,
    or who laid its cornerstone,
when the morning stars sang together,
    and all the sons of God shouted for joy? . . .

And the LORD said to Job:
"Shall a faultfinder contend with the Almighty?
    He who argues with God, let him answer it."

Then Job answered the LORD:
"Behold, I am of small account; what shall I answer
  thee?
  I lay my hand on my mouth.
I have spoken once, and I will not answer;
  twice, but I will proceed no further." . . .

Then Job answered the LORD:
"I know that thou canst do all things,
  and that no purpose of thine can be thwarted.
'Who is this that hides counsel without knowledge?'
Therefore I have uttered what I did not understand,
  things too wonderful for me, which I did not know.
'Hear, and I will speak;
  I will question you, and you declare to me.'
I had heard of thee by the hearing of the ear,
  but now my eye sees thee;
therefore I despise myself,
  and repent in dust and ashes."

JOB:
THE MAN
WHO COVERED
HIS MOUTH

AT FIRST I SAW NO POINT IN writing about Job's prayers. The prayers we have looked at so far all have a bearing on our own lives. But some prayers recorded in Scripture such as Job's do not seem to. They illustrate a direct encounter with God that overwhelms the person who experiences it.

Perhaps I should explain what I mean by a direct encounter. Already we have seen that God chooses to reveal himself to men not only in different ways but to different degrees. We are always in God's presence and may enjoy that fact as we exercise faith. But our conscious awareness of his presence may fluctuate according to a number of factors, the most important of which is the degree to which God chooses to disclose himself to us. Therefore while kneeling before the throne of grace I may know objectively that I am in God's presence, yet I may not experience subjectively anything more than quiet rejoicing.

Occasionally, however, God chooses to pull aside the veil

which conceals his glory from a man or woman. Christ did so before three of his disciples on the mount of transfiguration. Until the transfiguration Peter, James and John lived daily in the presence of the Lord of glory. They had learned from him; they had loved him. To be with him had sometimes cheered them and at other times convicted them. But all the while, though they thought that they knew him, his glory was veiled from them. Their reactions to its revelation on the mountain were profound. At that point, if I may express it very crudely, he became even more present in their experience than he had ever been before, and they were overwhelmed.

You can get some idea of the effects of such an encounter by thinking of a desert dweller catching his breath the first time he sees the ocean or of a city dweller suddenly placed atop the Matterhorn or of a jaded executive finding himself without warning resting among the silent beauties of coral reefs ten fathoms below the surface. Yet to encounter God may excite even more wonder, ecstasy, terror or shame than an exposure to his physical creation, however new or dramatic. John fell as if dead at the feet of the glorified Christ (Rev. 1:17). Daniel found "no strength . . . left in" him under similar circumstances (Dan. 10:8). Isaiah cried "Woe is me! For I am lost" (Is. 6:5). No one who has encountered God in such a way can ever forget what happened. It is a brightly colored page among the black and white of his biography.

People who write books about prayer commonly adopt one of two attitudes to direct encounters with God. They may ignore them altogether or they may represent them as true pearls to be sought above the costume jewelry of ordinary prayer. Writers who admire the mystics are sometimes in danger of following the latter course.

I would gladly have opted for the first alternative: to ignore the matter. It is simply not true that mystical experiences should be sought. John was not seeking a vision of his glorified Lord. Isaiah was, as far as we can tell, totally surprised by his encounter in the temple. I know of no one in Scripture who set out to have an experience of this type except Moses, and his encounter had already begun when he begged to see God's glory. God is the one who takes the initiative in communications between himself and his creatures. So if he should choose on occasion to come through on color TV rather than by mail or telephone, that is his business.

Since I have a practical turn of mind, I can see little point in lengthy discussions of experiences most of us will never have. Yet I feel that Job's prayer must be recorded in Scripture for a reason. There is something for us all, as well as for Job, in the experience. But what?

Intimacy's Counterfeit

One day we Christians will be physically transformed. Then, though there may be ecstasy when we experience God's immediacy, it will not overwhelm us in quite the same way it does now. At present, however, we can only stand so much. Having experienced a little in the way of such encounters, I would be terrified to ask what Moses asked. I know that my body and mind could not stand too much, however glorious the revelation might prove.

Why then should the Bible tell us anything about such matters? In what way are the experiences spiritually profitable? What happens to the person who reads about them? What happens to the person who undergoes them? The end result in my own life has not been any superior kind of spiritual state but a reverence and a holy fear such as I had not known before. And I believe that the biblical narratives let us catch vicarious glimpses to teach us such a reverence. It is my hope that something of what Job went through will rub off and affect our own attitude toward God. While we must never on the one hand lose the freedom to enter boldly and joyfully by faith into God's presence during our lives on earth, we must also learn how to revere God in our relationship with him.

We know little about reverence even in our human relationships. Some of our attempts at intimacy only cause antagonism between us and those we seek to be intimate with, so we have coined the dictum "familiarity breeds contempt." When we attempt intimacy we often go about it the wrong way. We confuse intimacy with its counterfeit, familiarity. Intimacy is what we want but familiarity is all we achieve. Intimacy is dangerous, a knowing and a being known deeply and profoundly. Casual familiarity may create the illusion of intimacy but it is much safer, having only to do with a pseudo-knowing.

The Galileans were familiar with Jesus. They did not know him; they only thought they knew him. They knew his parents. They had watched him grow up as a boy and had observed his developing skills as a carpenter. But their familiarity with him had blinded them to all that he really was. They had nonchalantly categorized him, putting him into the appropriate slot in their minds. Perhaps they had joked casually with him or teased him—their jokes or teasing based on the character they conceived him to have. Their familiarity was a familiarity of what they wanted to see, what they thought they saw.

"Oh yes, I know Jesus," one of them might have said. "Known him since he was a kid. Joseph's son, you know. Good carpenter. Nice kid. Bit quiet at times. Know him? I spoke to him practically every day of his life." They knew him so well in fact, that he could do no mighty work among them because of their unbelief.

Intimacy cannot occur without respect. And respect must be based on the fact that the one we desire intimacy with is a unique being created in God's image. We need to see more than physical appearance, to hear more than the sound of a voice or even the content of words spoken. We must see the living miracle of a being in whom the ongoing creativity of God is taking place—a masterpiece of his handiwork infinitely precious because God both made it in his image and redeemed it by death.

This is why spurious attempts at intimacy on a first name basis or on casual embraces at a cocktail party prove unsatisfying and boring. We may achieve familiarity while wearing our masks and while being indifferent to the wonder of another person's being. And since we see only what we want to see, and expose nothing but the image we want to project (be it pompous or self-pitying), we enter an alliance of mutual contempt.

Intimacy involves a true knowing. Familiarity is the illusion of knowing in which I see only what I want to see, only that part of a person that I can cope with.

The man who makes a sport of laying women knows none of the women he lies with. He knows their bodies. He knows a few of their reactions and can calculate precisely how to get what he wants from them. But his knowing is not intimacy. He cares little about their hopes, their inner fears, their longings, their joys. If they try to tell him, he will say, "Oh sure, honey, I often feel like that myself" or "Aw shucks. Forget it, sweetheart. You're not like that at all." He does not want true intimacy, only physical intimacy which by itself can breed contempt. As he leaves a woman he may say to himself, "Forget it, sweetheart, that was a waste of time. I'm sure not going to become your psychiatrist."

Many a husband or wife may have the same attitude. That which was intended to be a bridge to intimacy may lead to indifference, boredom or even contempt.

Parents may be familiar with their children and children with their parents without either ever truly knowing each other. For intimacy involves a respectful listening and a respectful hearing. It also involves being humble enough to share the secrets of your heart, provided you know that in doing so you will help the one you share with and not burden him.

People in Prayer

Unhappily we live in a day in which psychologists and sociologists are aware of our need for intimacy. T-groups and other encounter groups as well as the "sharing" of some Christians are attempts to achieve the intimacy we so crave. But we fail because we do not respect and do not reverence the handiwork of God in the person with whom we seek intimacy. We learn to be casual, familiar, but never truly intimate.

Celestial Chum

There is often a carry-over of this tendency to be too casual, even to be flippant, in modern approaches to prayer. God used to be a benign Granddad. Now he is becoming a Celestial Chum. We may be striving for honesty, openness, a break from ritual, stereotype and so on, all of which are good. Conversational prayer, for instance, can be a breakthrough for some people. But because we are human, we are tone deaf to awe.

Recently I conducted a prayer meeting for some Christian leaders. After Scripture reading and some sharing I suggested, "Let's spend time together in worship and adoration so that our requests will come into perspective as we remind ourselves of the majesty of God." They all nodded eagerly, but it was clear from their prayers that no one had understood.

"Thank you, Lord, for the privilege we have in approaching you," ran one prayer. "Thank you for your many blessings. Please help us, O Lord, to be obedient to you. Bless the services in the church and grant that. . . ." Or someone else would pray, "Thank you, Lord, for reminding us that we ought to worship you more. Forgive us for our failure to do this. Forgive us also for not being more loving to one another. Help us to be more faithful day by day, witnessing by our lips as well as by our lives. Bless the many missionaries. . . ."

Thanksgiving, yes. Praise for practical things, even for spiritual blessings. But with a sinking heart I realized that those who prayed were blind to the majesty and glory of God.

Job: The Man Who Covered His Mouth

I could not be critical of such prayers. But it was obvious to me that had the Christian leaders been granted a vision of a glorified Lord, the content of their prayers would have been more God-centered. Their prayers might have been, "Lord, as we see you as you are, we marvel that you are interested in us at all. We are overwhelmed by your glory. We can only say, 'Worthy are you, O Lord, to receive honor, praise, dominion and power.' We fall on our faces before you and are delighted to know that we are creatures of your creating, slaves by you redeemed. Your love is incomparable and we have no words to magnify it enough." Let us have a look at Job's prayer, that the Holy Spirit may remind us that we need to learn to tremble, as well as to be close.

Death-Wish Road

No one is really sure how old the book is, but certainly it is one of the oldest in Scripture. Some scholars suggest that original-ly it simply contained the tale of the first two chapters and the last part of chapter 42. They contend that a later author com-posed the intervening chapters. This middle portion, the bulk of the book, uses superbly poetic language to recount the pas-sionate discussion of the meaning of Job's tragedy. Be that as it may, it is a book inspired by the Holy Spirit.

Job was a good man who honored God and was rewarded by God. Yet in response to Satan's cynicism about Job, God allows Satan to inflict whatever pain he wishes, provided only that Job's life be spared. As a result a series of catastrophes overwhelm Job. He loses his fortune, his children, his health and even the respect and support of his wife. Wretched, in pain and profoundly depressed, he refuses either to despair or to curse God and die. His friends exhort him to recognize that his difficulties are the result of his sin. God is never to blame, they say. Therefore the blame must be Job's.

These middle chapters are heavy going for most people. They used to be for me. I read the book through dutifully several times years ago, and I'm sure I learned something from it. But the memory is vague. More recently, reading it in the New English Bible, I couldn't put the book down. I was gripped by the majesty and beauty of the language, the slow revelation of the characters of the three friends, their bitter intransigence and Job's adamant refusal to accept their verdict.

It is too simple to dismiss the book by saying it deals with the problem of suffering. It is a heart-rending account of a man in the depth of despair who cannot believe that God is punishing him; or if God is doing so, he believes God would stop if he could hear his side of the story. In the face of the trite and even hostile accusations of his so-called friends and their pedantic repetition of things, Job already knows, in grief, pain, bereavement and abandonment, he can yet rise to a peak of affirmation because at the heart of the universe will ultimately lie justice and therefore his personal vindication before God and the world.

But in his tenacity he comes dangerously close to saying he is right, and he will get God to admit it if he can. Can we blame him? Who among us could take the battering Job took? For Job there were only two routes to go: the one of bitterness and despair (the route he was beginning to tread when his friends found him) or the route of angry self-justification.

So your friends in fact did you a service, Job. By inciting you to righteous indignation and sarcasm they drove you off the death-wish road of meaninglessness to one of rage and at one point almost of burning joy. You swell in the course of the book to a hero of epic proportions. In some way your God comes across as smaller than you. (Who was it that without your consent casually tossed you into the malicious hands of Satan, just to prove a point?) Did he not admit, at the very outset, that you were indeed an unusually righteous man?

Yet when your chance came to question, what did he say to you? It was, "I have some questions to ask you first, Job. You do not really know enough to become my judge. Let me remind you who we both are" (see Job 38:1-3; 40:1-2). And from your response it is clear that you saw him as well as heard him. You were humbled—how you were humbled—but you were at peace and in your right mind again.

Small Is Healthy
How did Job respond?

"I lay my hand upon my mouth." Suddenly the previous torrent of words seemed pointless, empty. They were redundant, out of place. They could add nothing to what he now saw. Words were as superfluous as some pinhead's typewritten comments about art, Scotchtaped to the Pietà or the Mona Lisa. Job knew as never before that he who meets God does indeed have nothing to say. How can one amplify the content of omniscience or formulate a critique on burning holiness?

"I am of small account." It is comforting to be reduced to size. I think of the time I entered Ely Cathedral, stark in its naked simplicity, yet awe-inspiring beyond words. My heart stood still before an upward sweep of towering Gothic arches, light and the beauty of space. It was good to feel small, good because something so great made being small at once fitting and uplifting. One cannot simultaneously be *puffed* up and *lifted* up.

For Job, of course, it was the same thing on another level. He experienced smallness in every sense: morally, intellectually and physically in the presence of majesty. It was painful because he was shattered by his stupid folly. Yet we are never at home when we swell with importance. We may think we are having a high, but if so, it is a high never free from burdens and tensions. We may be hurt to see our real size for the first time, though in seeing it we will be delivered from the burden of having to keep our bloated image up to size. Being big became to Job as unnecessary as speech had become.

There is something both profoundly healthy and holy

about being small and reduced to silence. Nowadays we lay great stress on having a proper self-image. We rightly see that feelings of inferiority can hamper the way we live. To feel that we are no good gives us a hangdog, self-hating attitude toward life. We therefore seek to correct such a state of affairs by having an "improved self-image," by which we usually mean a bigger and better idea of ourselves. Supposedly, we are to look in the mirror and be impressed by what we see.

Yet is this how God intends it? It seems to me that the real problem of having a poor self-image (or, in more old-fashioned terms, "an inferiority complex") lies in self-disgust. It really does not matter how small we are, but how at peace we are with ourselves. And he is at peace who has seen himself appropriately placed in the total scheme of things. The problem is not that we are small but that we are competitive and therefore displaced persons in the mad scramble for a place in life. Consequently we grow resentful of others, resentful even of God. We tread in the footsteps of Lucifer. We are children seeing who is the tallest, but we are measuring ourselves by false and shifting standards.

To know that we are small yet accepted and loved, and that we fit into the exact niche in life a loving God has carved out for us is the most profoundly healthy thing I know. It does not inhibit boldness or assertiveness when these are called for, and it certainly delivers us from silly, aggressive posturing and shouting. Knowing our real place in life we never need to feel threatened. Most of all we are left free to wonder at the glory and majesty of God, drinking in drafts of living water and knowing what we are created for.

Sounds of Silence
Small and speechless.

Yet Job *must* speak. Had his words been taped I doubt they would have come out gracefully and smoothly—rather incoherently and chokingly. "I know that thou canst do all things, and that no purpose of thine can be thwarted." He had to say it. He wanted to say it. Suddenly saying words of that sort became the sublimest gift that life could offer. He was not only seeing God but was seizing the high glory of praising him. And whether he wept, choked or had his beard matted with mucus, he *had* to get the words out. What else could he do at the sight of such effulgence?

" Who is this that hides counsel without knowledge?" (He is quoting God's opening question of Job 38:2.) "Therefore I have uttered what I did not understand, things too wonderful for me, which I did not know." He laughs at himself through his tears. It is good to laugh in the presence of God at our own imbecility. Tears and laughter are mingled, for nothing matters anymore when one finds oneself there and discovers with amazement that one can still breathe.

" 'Hear, and I will speak; I will question you, and you declare to me.' " Once again he is repeating in self-mockery the words of God himself (Job 40:7). "I had heard of thee by the hearing of the ear, but now my eye sees thee." Observe the distinction. He had not heard God. He had heard *about* him. Now all is changed. He both hears and sees him.

And what did he see? I think he would find that part very difficult to explain. He might say, "It was as if . . . it was like, . . ." and then shake his head. You get this same feeling in reading Ezekiel and John in the Apocalypse when they struggle to describe the indescribable. The description is actually beside the point. He knew that immediacy we were talking about earlier. Whatever God looked like, Job and God were right there together. He saw a whirlwind, but it was like no whirlwind you ever saw and it made him most happy to say, "therefore I . . . repent in dust and ashes."

Repent? He has changed completely. The man who outtalked three self-righteous windbags and remained obdurately convinced of his ultimate vindication, now repents. He knows he has been wrong. He feels it intensely and admits it freely. He almost seems to go too far. Dust and ashes. A metaphor perhaps? Or would Job really put dust and ashes upon his head in token of his abasement? Does Job sound as if he is groveling?

Do you despise people who grovel? Perhaps you don't understand. What you hate is obsequiousness. When a man gets in the dust before God he is not currying favor. That was the last thing in Job's mind. His repentance was worship. The dust and ashes were as appropriate as a bridal kiss (and a good deal more passionate). Certainly self-horror and self-loathing were present too. But the whirlwind would make short shrift of them. You cannot retain self-loathing in the presence of glory, for the glory burns it all away.

A Richness Greater Than Riches
Reverence.

Perhaps if you begin to catch even a vicarious glimpse of awesomeness, you may also begin to understand its relevance. It can be practiced deliberately when you pray, "Hallowed be thy name," as Jesus taught us to say. It is immaterial whether you ever tangle with a whirlwind. And, as I have already warned, it is probably not the wisest thing to go looking for one. What matters is that God should receive from you the worship that such a God merits. It is his due. You are indebted to offer it. Be still by faith in his presence. Acknowledge in words that he is very God of very God, that every breath that fills your lungs comes from him, that no one else is worthy to rule the universe. Tell him that you know he is holy and that there is no one like him. Tell him that you owe him your allegiance, your body, your time. Tell him that you recognize that his mercy to you is far more than you ever deserve. The Holy Spirit will teach you how to go on.

Job's story has a happy ending. God was not reacting to Job out of pride nor was his speech from the whirlwind a haughty put-down. God's correction was designed to restore Job's perspective, indeed to improve it. And it is plain that Job retained God's warm approval (Job 42:7).

At the end of the book we find his relationship with his friends has been reversed. He now becomes the one who is to plead with God for their forgiveness. Job is vindicated not by his righteousness but by God's mercy while his friends are condemned.

The fact that he had twice as much property and twice as many children at the end of the story may mean little to us. We are inclined to be supercilious about stories which end, "And they all lived happily ever after." Yet in an age when such things (prosperity, children) were seen as signs of divine approval, they were meant to tell us that pain is not necessarily punishment. Those whom God loves may indeed undergo trials which need not imply sin or divine wrath.

The problem of suffering remains incompletely solved in the book, but for Job it no longer existed. It was not just that his fortunes were restored again. A greater richness had come into his life, the richness a man knows when he treasures the majesty and glory of God. Such riches breed deep contentment and Job eventually died "an old man, and full of days" (Job 42:17).

8

**2 Samuel
6:1-23**

David again gathered all the chosen men of Israel,
thirty thousand. And David arose and went with all the
people who were with him from Baale-judah, to bring
up from there the ark of God, which is called by the
name of the LORD of hosts who sits enthroned on the
cherubim. And they carried the ark of God upon a
new cart, and brought it out of the house of Abinadab
which was on the hill; and Uzzah and Ahio, the sons of
Abinadab, were driving the new cart with the ark of
God, and Ahio went before the ark. And David and all
the house of Israel were making merry before the
LORD with all their might, with songs and lyres and
harps and tambourines and castanets and cymbals.

And when they came to the threshing floor of
Nacon, Uzzah put out his hand to the ark of God and
took hold of it, for the oxen stumbled. And the anger
of the LORD was kindled against Uzzah; and God
smote him there because he put forth his hand to the
ark; and he died there beside the ark of God. And
David was angry because the LORD had broken forth
upon Uzzah; and that place is called Perez-uzzah, to
this day. And David was afraid of the LORD that
day; and he said, "How can the ark of the LORD
come to me?" So David was not willing to take the
ark of the LORD into the city of David; but David
took it aside to the house of Obed-edom the Gittite. And
the ark of the LORD remained in the house of Obed-
edom the Gittite three months; and the LORD blessed
Obed-edom and all his household.

And it was told King David, "The LORD has
blessed the household of Obed-edom and all that belongs to him, because of the ark of God." So David
went and brought up the ark of God from the house of
Obed-edom to the city of David with rejoicing; and

when those who bore the ark of the LORD had gone six paces, he sacrificed an ox and a fatling. And David danced before the LORD with all his might; and David was girded with a linen ephod. So David and all the house of Israel brought up the ark of the LORD with shouting, and with the sound of the horn.

As the ark of the LORD came into the city of David, Michal the daughter of Saul looked out of the window, and saw King David leaping and dancing before the LORD; and she despised him in her heart. And they brought in the ark of the LORD, and set it in its place, inside the tent which David had pitched for it; and David offered burnt offerings and peace offerings before the LORD. And when David had finished offering the burnt offerings and the peace offerings, he blessed the people in the name of the LORD of hosts, and distributed among all the people, the whole multitude of Israel, both men and women, to each a cake of bread, a portion of meat, and a cake of raisins. Then all the people departed, each to his house.

And David returned to bless his household. But Michal the daughter of Saul came out to meet David, and said, "How the king of Israel honored himself today, uncovering himself today before the eyes of his servants' maids, as one of the vulgar fellows shamelessly uncovers himself!" And David said to Michal, "It was before the LORD, who chose me above your father, and above all his house, to appoint me as prince over Israel, the people of the LORD—and I will make merry before the LORD. I will make myself yet more contemptible than this, and I will be abased in your eyes; but by the maids of whom you have spoken, by them I shall be held in honor." And Michal the daughter of Saul had no child to the day of her death.

DAVID:
THE LORD
AND THE DANCE

PRAYER HAS A BROADER MEANING than merely talking
with God, covering as it does a wide range of divine/human
interactions. Some modern approaches to prayer startle the
more conservative among us. Raised hands, tapping feet,
strummed guitars, swaying bodies, clacking castanets, rattling
maracas, snapping fingers and clashing timbrels all characterize the modern church scene. Barefoot girls with long
hair and long dresses flow sinuously together in sacred dance.
Although much of what I describe is given the broader appel-
lation *worship* rather than the narrower term *prayer*, there are
issues common to both that must be resolved.

Advocates of freer worship, many but not all of whom form
part of the charismatic movement, point to the references to
dance (which implies rhythm as well as melody) in the Old
Testament. Perhaps we should look at two chapters there,
both from the books of Samuel, concerning ourselves less with
the form prayer takes than with the *attitudes* underlying the

form. In particular let us look at two attitudes which must always be present in combination: rejoicing and reverence. Sound and movement will thus be seen as less important than what gave rise to them.

First, we must again familiarize ourselves with the background of the passages we are dealing with. I shall begin by painting four scenarios, three of them from the passages that head the chapter.

God's Portable Shrine

Two cows yoked to a crude cart are pulling a treasure of the ancient world now lost to archaeology. The cloth wrappings which should cover so sacred an object are missing. It is overlaid with gold. The afternoon sun gleams from the outspread wings of two cherubim facing each other from either end of the lid of an oblong gold box. The box is about four feet long with ends two and a half feet square.

Wonderingly, a huge crowd of people slowly follows the cows. Philistine princes, priests, peasants, warriors, men, women and perhaps children seem strangely awed and subdued. And well they might be. Before their eyes a miracle is apparently taking place, a miracle climaxing months of uncanny events which have terrorized the Philistines and made them respect and fear the God who is supposed to dwell invisibly between the cherubim.

The strange events began when the Philistines captured what we now know as the ark of the covenant (or the ark of the Lord) in battle with the Israelites. They deposited the sacred object in the temple of their god Dagon. Dagon and the ark faced each other overnight in the sacred precincts and the next morning Dagon's astonished priests found their god lying face down before the ark. Dismayed, they put him back in his place. But the morning after they were yet more troubled to find Dagon face down and smashed. The body lay prostrate on the platform while the head and arms had crashed to the stone floor below.

Dagon's temple lay in the city of Ashdod and for the next several months Ashdodites became the unhappy subjects of outbreaks of sickness and a plague of rats. Everyone in Philistia was sure that the hostile alien deity was behind the evil and a new respect for this God began to grow in their hearts. Priests and soothsayers were summoned and consulted.

Several measures were adopted. First an indemnity was to be paid to the God of Israel for the indignities he had suffered. A gold rat and a gold "tumor" (scholars are uncertain of the form of illness the Ashdodites suffered) were given by each of the five city-states that made up Philistia. The gold objects were placed alongside the ark on a new cart with the gold-covered poles on which the ark was normally carried. A pair of cows never before yoked were then selected. They had to be milch cows, cows nursing their calves. The mothers were to be forcibly separated from their calves, yoked to the cart and then set free to go wherever they wanted.

The source of all the strange instructions is unknown. By what process did the experts in magic arrive at their bizarre conclusions? Yet as the instructions were followed, the miracle began.

Lowing pitifully, bereft of their calves, the cows dragged their burden slowly toward the border with Israel. Cows that have never experienced the yoke normally struggle. The strange new burden frightens them. Each could be predicted to pull a different way with the common intent of escaping the unfamiliar and the fearful. Even if they had remained calm, which would have been most unusual, they would under normal circumstances have been too preoccupied with the loss of their young to go anywhere. Indeed we know that they were so preoccupied. The detail of their pitiful moaning tells us this.

Five Philistine princes and an untold number of others were present as the priests' instructions were carried out. We are given no details. Perhaps the cows moved uncertainly at first, now stopping, now starting again. Or perhaps there was no hesitation at all. Perhaps they walked as directly as a crow is alleged to fly. And when they walked, the crowd of Philistines followed in eerie, fascinated procession.

What were they following? Portable shrines (the ark was a portable shrine) were common enough in the ancient world. From between the cherubim hovering over the gold lid (called the mercy seat) God spoke with his servants. Beneath the lid lay certain objects: a pot of manna, Aaron's famous budding rod and the tablets containing the Decalogue. The Decalogue made the ark unique among all other shrines in the Middle East. Here was no idol. The invisible God chose to dwell and to meet with his people where his revealed will and written promises were kept in sacred memory.

Slowly the cart was drawn across the border. God did not need to be recaptured by the Israelites. He had brought his awe-struck captors back like prisoners in a conqueror's train.

Rejoicing Turned to Terror

The late afternoon sun shone on a golden valley where a great rock rose from among the wheat. The men, women and children of Beth-shemesh were reaping their harvest. Suddenly a cry aroused the reapers. They looked up to see a strange sight. Excited cries echoed around the valley. Cows were pulling a cart toward them. They instantly recognized the ark of God. Slowly on the ridge of the hill a crowd of Philistines appeared, watching awhile from the distance before turning back home.

The harvest was forgotten. Within an hour the cart was hewn in pieces, the cows butchered and the rock of Beth-shemesh transformed into an improvised altar. The reapers laughed and sang for joy as for the first time in months they made a sacrifice before their Lord.

What happened next is not clear. Some translations of the

Bible accuse certain men of Beth-shemesh of trying to look inside the ark. Newer translations with access to a wider selection of ancient manuscripts simply state that certain men, unlike the rest of the people, "did not rejoice." Something, whatever it was, went wrong. Without any warning seventy of the local men died.

In a moment the air of festivity died away. Dismay and fear settled like a cloud over the valley "The people mourned," we read, "because the LORD had made a great slaughter among the people" (1 Sam. 6:19). Their fear led to alienation from God. Danger had reared its head among them. The ark had proved to be no magic talisman; their divine protector could also be their judge. They could no more possess or own him than the Philistines could, and who wanted to have such an unpredictable Being around?

In the end God was sent into exile to a place called Kiriath-jearim where the Gibeonites lived. A keeper was appointed to take care of him, almost as though he were some dangerous beast, while "all the house of Israel lamented after the LORD" (1 Sam. 7:2). They went on lamenting for twenty years. And even then they did not understand.

Death and Good Fortune

The lamentation finally ended. David and a whole host of people set out to bring the ark from its "keepers" to Jerusalem. As the procession returned, there began a celebration such as Israel had never seen before. Music filled the air, the music of singing and of instruments. Laughter bubbled up breathlessly between the notes as dancers flung limbs and bodies in frenzied abandon of joy. God was coming home to his sanctuary. No one danced with greater abandon than David the King.

Music, song, laughter, dance—all were expressions of praise and joy to the Lord. They fit in little with our more conventional idea of prayer, and may heaven forbid that they should be the only form of prayer. Prayer can be broken weeping as well as joyful dancing. It can groan as well as sing. It can question, reason, plead, argue or bow in silence. But here we are dealing with prayer as dancing, plucked strings, clanging tambourines and song.

All went well until the tired crowd began to rest for the night by a farm. As the cart (a new cart) was hauled onto the threshing floor it rocked so that the ark tipped perilously. Uzzah, one of its keepers, shot out his hand to prevent it from falling. Instantly he died.

It seemed as though the history of twenty years past was repeating itself. Once the initial commotion subsided a solemnity and quietness spread through the weary crowd. David himself was furious and bitter. He was also scared. All desire to dance left his limbs. His great project had ended in tragedy and humiliation.

The ark was left in the house of a man named Obed-edom the Gittite, and the revelers returned empty-handed to Jerusalem. but as the crowds departed, a new joy and a new prosperity began to attend the house of Obed-edom, and for three months his good fortune continued.

The End of a Marriage

What made David change his mind and go back for the ark? Certainly the news of Obed-edom's prosperity must have caused him to think. But what guarantee did he have that further tragedy would not strike? What reason lay behind the awful rage of God? How could anyone be sure it would not break out again? Had I been in David's shoes I would have gone trembling to fetch the ark. There would have been no music, no dancing, only bowed heads and a solemn, reverent walk.

In actual fact one little change took place. There was sacrifice offered before the party set out the second time, but it is not to this I refer. Sacrifices had been offered in Beth-shemesh, yet seventy men had died. The difference was that the ark this time was to be carried on the shoulders of men, not driven like an exhibit at a fair or like the ancient equivalent of a float (see 2 Sam. 6:13).

Why is the difference so important? The ark was never meant to be driven on a cart. Careful instructions had been issued in the Levitical Laws. The gold-covered poles, fitting through the rings in the lower corners of the ark, were designed for the shoulders of the Levites. You drive a cart. You are driven, so to speak, when you bear the sacred presence on your shoulders.

Hundreds of years before God had led his people across the river Jordan, while the ark was borne by the priests as God led the way into the turbulent waters (see Josh. 3:1-6). Borne on human shoulders, God was in control. Bearing God on their shoulders, people show their reverence for him, their submission to him. The horse is the obedient servant of the rider and the more powerful the rider, the more subservient the horse.

It was a little thing, but it spelled a great difference in the relation between God and humanity. God was neither being featured as an exhibit nor possessed as a talisman, but was ruling over and guiding his subjects.

I have no doubt that the lesson of reverence had gone home to David's heart, but David could see that reverence and rejoicing were compatible. So music sounded again, singers poured out their hearts in melody, and David led the dancers from the house of Obed-edom to Jerusalem in a wild, leaping dance of abandoned joy.

As the trumpets sounded and the exuberant procession passed below the palace windows, Michal, David's wife, bit her lips in shame. More crowds gathered. More offerings were made. Food was distributed among the people. The whole population dispersed to their homes, tired, grateful and content. But a scornful wife met David in his own home.

Her eyes flashed and she spat derision at him. She claimed he had made a cheap exhibition of himself.

Their relationship, always turbulent, ended there and then.

Spiritual Pornography

Was Michal right? Had the dancing, the music, the wild abandon been no more than a display of human disinhibition? Had men and women been behaving like savages, even like beasts in an orgy which had nothing to do with true prayer?

David did not think so. "It was before the LORD," he stated categorically, " . . . and I will make merry before the LORD." Nor, if you examine the passages I have been summarizing, is there any evidence that the disinhibited praise offended God. It might not have been compatible with some people's ideas of dignity, but who should be concerned with *our* dignity before the Most High? It is God's dignity that matters. And God's dignity consists in his innate worth and majesty, not in his capacity to disguise his deepest emotions. The dignity that can only be maintained by always concealing what I feel, is not dignity. It is known as being a stuffed shirt. We were not made in the image of a Stuffed Shirt.

I am British by birth and breeding, so that stuffiness in my shirts is resistive to the wash. In meetings where people feel led by the Spirit to lift their hands, I find I have rheumatic shoulders. I could no more dance in the Spirit than I could be a trapeze artist. Yet I know that when due allowance has been made for fads, for bandwagon followers and for phonies, there are those to whom God's Spirit gives the grace to praise him in just the way David did. It was not against rejoicing, even against abandoned expressions of rejoicing that God's rage was (and still is) awakened. In fact if we pay heed to the greatest weight of scholarship it was for *want* of rejoicing that the seventy men of Beth-shemesh were slain.

I began this chapter by suggesting that two attitudes must be combined when we approach God in prayer, whatever form the prayer may take: rejoicing and reverence. The absence of rejoicing, especially when rejoicing is appropriate, is sin. Cold indifference toward God or resentment toward him can in his presence become like droplets of water in a furnace, scorched into oblivion. We are to approach him with gratitude, with praise and with thanksgiving.

But rejoicing without reverence becomes spiritual pornography, and we live in such an age. Those of us who are not charismatics have our own irreverent ways of rejoicing before the Lord. We have song leaders with white teeth who urge on us our duty to smile. We are called upon to make the rafters ring to our singing and at times we do in fact experience enjoyment both of the melodies and the meaning of the songs we sing. We begin to rejoice. As we learned in the chapter on Job, we need as never before to learn reverence in our rejoicing.

Reverence begins with fear, though reverence and fear are not synonymous. Fear may be a gateway leading us to reverence, but the two must not be confused.

Fear in the passages we have been examining arose in response to the wrath of God. God's rage in Beth-shemesh provoked such a fear of him that the inhabitants sent the ark away. This in itself shows us how very different the effects of fear and reverence are. Fear alienates us from God. Reverence brings us trembling to his feet. His anger against Uzzah (2 Sam. 6:7) made David, by turns, both angry himself (2 Sam. 6:8) and afraid (2 Sam. 6:9).

Whereas we can tolerate the idea of reverence for God, it appalls us that fear should be the instrument by which reverence is learned, and it appalls us even more that God's anger was what evidently awoke the fear. We are dismayed alike by the idea of fear in ourselves and of anger in God. In part we are confused because we think God's anger is like our own whereas nothing could be further from the truth.

My anger, for instance, often arises from impatience. My

pencil breaks. I put it in the pencil sharpener but the lead snaps off just as I get it to a fine point. The same thing happens a second time. I get mad. I am in a hurry and my patience gives way. God is never in a hurry. Broken pencils never bother him.

At other times I grow angry because I am weak and powerless. The government, the boss, the income tax authorities all get at me in ways which give me no comeback. I fuss and fume because there is nothing I can do. I honk my horn in a traffic jam because I am powerless to shift the cars that hem me in. God has no need to fuss and fume. He is never frustrated. He is almighty. There is nothing that can ever resist his will.

I have seen men angry because they are afraid. God is never afraid. I have seen men angry because they dare not speak their mind. They are scared of saying to their wives exactly what they feel, so they kick the dog instead. God speaks his Word with no thought of fear. He has no need to vent his spleen on the innocent.

What then is God's anger? It is an implacable hostility to all that is evil. Though sometimes we read of God's wrath being "kindled," the Bible is really using a figure of speech. For God's anger is fixed. It is absolute, immutable, eternal. It is part of himself. He could not remain God and cease his irrevocable rage against evil. He is angry because he is God, just as he is love because he is God. He is angry with corrupt government, with cruelty, oppression, violence, terrorism, exploitation and all the wickedness by which man does evil to man.

But he restrains the expression of his anger. He is longsuffering in judgment. And when his anger is displayed he has a serious purpose in displaying it.

But why should he make men afraid? We are foolish to suppose that fear is evil. Fear can be either good or bad according to its effect upon us. A child's fear of fire can lead to a healthy respect for its destructive powers, a respect which enables the child in later life to make wise use of fire's benefits. Without fear the child could be severly burned. It would be better for the child to be so terrified that he never made use of fire, than for him to be destroyed by fire. But it is better still that the child, through fear, learn that degree of respect which enables him to harness fire's power.

Fear, then, is a steppingstone to enrichment in our spiritual life. Without fear we are exposed to dangers of which we have little or no understanding. If through fear we learn reverence for God, our feet will be set on the road that leads to wisdom.

Of one thing we may be sure. God did not lose his temper either with Uzzah or with the men of Beth-shemesh. There was a reason why he allowed his anger to be expressed at such times and in such a way. On both occasions a salutary effect eventually followed. The people of Israel learned that their God was the God high above all. He was not a talisman. They did not own him as a national resource. He was "their" God only in the sense that he had graciously chosen them, not they him. Neither Uzzah nor the seventy of Beth-shemesh had been unjustly treated. Every one of them deserved death a thousand times over. In his mercy God allowed his just judgments upon them to awaken Israel in general and David in particular to something they all badly needed to know: that God is God, and humans are human; and that God's presence in their midst was a privilege a human race will never deserve and must never take for granted.

It is evident from a reading of the psalms that David had already been awakened to this fact in the past. But he had forgotten it. The death of Uzzah served as a shocking reminder to him of who and what God is. So as the months passed and the reassuring news of Obed-edom's blessing reached him, fear gave place to reverence, and with reverence, joy was awakened again. Pornography gave place to adoration.

Dance if you want before the Lord Jehovah. Sing his praises with an abandoned joy. Be merry in his presence and clap

People in Prayer

your hands. Let your guitars sound their melodies and your castanets their rhythm. Stomp your feet and sway your body.

But remember you are in the presence of the Most High God. He gives you breath. He holds your pulsing heart between his fingers. His rage against evil will never cease. It does not harm you because in your case it is assuaged by the blood of his only Son. And for his sake he welcomes you with love. Let your rejoicing then be with reverence and with godly fear.

9

**Ephesians
1:11-23;
3:14-21**

In him, according to the purpose of him who accomplishes all things according to the counsel of his will, we who first hoped in Christ have been destined and appointed to live for the praise of his glory. In him you also, who have heard the word of truth, the gospel of your salvation, and have believed in him, were sealed with the promised Holy Spirit, which is the guarantee of our inheritance until we acquire possession of it, to the praise of his glory.

For this reason, because I have heard of your faith in the Lord Jesus and your love toward all the saints, I do not cease to give thanks for you, remembering you in my prayers, that the God of our Lord Jesus Christ, the Father of glory, may give you a spirit of wisdom and of revelation in the knowledge of him, having the eyes of your hearts enlightened, that you may know what is the hope to which he has called you, what are the riches of his glorious inheritance in the saints, and what is the immeasurable greatness of his power in us who believe, according to the working of his great might which he accomplished in Christ when he raised him from the dead and made him sit at his right hand in the heavenly places, far above all rule and authority and power and dominion, and above every name that is named, not only in this age but also in that which is to come; and he has put all things under his feet and has made him the head over all things for the church, which is his body, the fulness of him who fills all in all.

For this reason I bow my knees before the Father, from whom every family in heaven and on earth is named, that according to the riches of his glory he may grant you to be strengthened with might through his Spirit in the inner man, and that Christ may dwell in your hearts through faith; that you, being rooted and grounded in love, may have power to comprehend with all the saints what is the breadth and length and height and depth, and to know the love of Christ which surpasses knowledge, that you may be filled with all the fulness of God.

Now to him who by the power at work within us is able to do far more abundantly than all that we ask or think, to him be glory in the church and in Christ Jesus to all generations, for ever and ever. Amen.

PAUL:
PRAYING
FOR OTHERS

PAUL'S LETTER TO THE EPHESIANS consists of a two-part prayer, boxed in theology, wrapped in exhortations and tied with love. I have a feeling (not shared by commentators or New Testament scholars) that the prayer is the nodal point around which the whole letter turns. Paul's introduction leads up to the prayer. In the middle of the prayer he gets sidetracked, bemused by the wonder of the Christ about whom he speaks (Eph. 1:20-23); but halfway through the letter he tries to get back to it (Eph. 3:1), only to be sidetracked again. Not until chapter 3 verse 14 does he finally settle down and finish telling the Ephesians how and what he is praying. The exhortations that complete the letter are exhortations we can make only after we have prayed as Paul did.

Now while I see the prayer as the kernel of the nut and the rest of the epistle as the shell, I must not press the point too far. The theology and the exhortation are of undeniable importance. Yet as I read the letter it seems as though an excited

People in Prayer

Paul tosses such jewels in by way of explaining why he prays what he prays. To many of us the jewels themselves are primary. I suspect that to Paul they were secondary.

The prayer differs from prayers we have looked at so far. It is once removed from us. Instead of actually overhearing Paul in prayer we read a letter in which he describes his prayer for the Ephesians. But the prayer loses little in the retelling.

"For this reason . . ." he writes. For which reason? Paul has just mentioned a dozen possible reasons for prayer and immediately goes on to assert that he prays because he heard of their faith and love. If he is not referring to the faith and love of those he prays for, to which of the many facts that he mentions in the introduction to his epistle does he refer?

The Fuel and the Flame

The why is important. It is important because we ourselves often have a tough time getting down to prayer. Prayer can be relatively easy when we come fresh from an exhilarating conference or when we have read an interesting book about the subject or even when we find ourselves in a crisis with serious problems which makes us aware of our need for divine help. But day-by-day intercession (prayer for others) month in, month out, often becomes a weariness. Paul evidently found it to be less so than some of us. In his eagerness words tumble over one another. He seems excited to share with the Ephesians how glad he is to pray for them. Why? Because the flames of prayer were leaping in his heart, feeding as they did on the fuel of truth.

Prayer is a fire which needs fuel to burn and a match to light it. If the fire burns low we can fan it so that the flame may burn more fiercely. But all the fanning in the world cannot create a bonfire from a single match nor from a pile of dead, cold fuel.

Fire must come from above; indeed he has already come. The Holy Spirit burns quietly within the Christian ready to light the fuel of Scripture's truth. But the fuel must be there.

Paul: Praying for Others

In Paul's case it is evident that his mind was so soaked in divine truth that it served as the fuel by which his prayers caught on fire. In the first three chapters of the epistle he has, as we have already noted, a difficult time getting down to describing the prayer itself because of his preoccupation with truths about Christ. Yet in expressing these same truths he gives away his secret, for the truths are the fuel which burns in his prayers. As the Holy Spirit had drawn Paul's attention to what God was doing in Ephesus, there had been an explosion of flame in Paul. The fagots of truth came alive and prayer was born. Had the fuel not been there he would not have had the wherewithal to pray, for the Holy Spirit does not by preference inflame an empty heart but rather an instructed mind. We are conscious collaborators and partners in prayer, not blind instruments.

If we would intercede for others, then we must soak our minds in Scripture that the Holy Spirit may have fuel to light within us. There must be plenty of fuel, not just isolated texts chosen at random. The fuel has to be thick and heavy. Promises may catch alight quickly, but for a lasting fire we will need some solid knowledge about the nature and the character of God and of his Christ and of their intervention in human history. Straw may produce a brilliant flash, but we will need logs for sustained burning.

Let me put the matter another way. We cannot pray fervently without faith and hope. If we approach a door expecting that no one will be at home or fearing that whoever is at home will receive us coldly, we may not be inclined to knock more than once. On the other hand the fact that we may have been received with frequent kindness will give us the faith and hope to knock hard a second time. And in the same way, faith and hope in God bring prayer alive and make it persistent. Both virtues, faith and hope, come to us in the measure that Scripture is stored in our minds and hearts. If then we want to know what it means to have prayers that burn with hope, or if, putting it another way, we want to knock on the door expectantly, we will need a mind molded by Scripture.

I must not leave the impression that we should only pray when we burn in blessed ecstacy. We may need to fan the flames of prayer, even to fan them long and hard. We are not excused from duty because our feelings do not accommodate themselves to it.

Yet at the same time I must be careful to express clearly what I mean by fanning the flames of prayer since forcing ourselves into a phony fervor can be soul-destroying, crippling and God-dishonoring. Why fan if there is nothing to burn?

Fanning the flames, then, means meditating upon Scripture, affirming our confidence before God in its reliability, praising him for its content and asking him whether the truths we meditate on do not indeed apply to those for whom we pray. It may please the Holy Spirit on occasion to cause a sudden uprush of flame from the material, so that fanning becomes unnecessary. The fuel in other words may or may not need to be fanned, but the fuel must be present if it is to burn.

We saw in Daniel's prayer how God had taken the initiative by awakening Daniel through Scripture. Evidently the same is true of Paul. In Daniel the Word produced tension while in Paul it produced delight, but the end result was the same in both men: they prayed.

It may be important to ask, Given that Scripture truth is in general fuel for the flames of prayer, what particular truths incited Paul to pray? A glance at Ephesians 1:11-15 gives us at least a partial answer. I will summarize the verses since they may have a bearing on our own prayer lives: God had a purpose for the Ephesians. It was his plan that they should live "for the praise of his glory." God had given the Holy Spirit to the Ephesians, thereby guaranteeing that his plan would be carried out. Already there was evidence in the lives of the

Ephesians that the Holy Spirit had been at work.

If we are praying for fellow Christians, we should ask ourselves the following questions: Who was it that rescued them from death? What did he have in mind in doing so? Who wrote their names in the Lamb's book of life? Who gave them his Spirit as a guarantee of their sonship? Who lives forever to make intercession for them? Who has promised that the work he begins is a work he intends to complete (Phil. 1:6)? We must pause and turn our attention upon him before opening our mouths. We may not be the world's mightiest prayer warriors, but it helps to consider: How does God feel toward the person we pray for? What investment does God have in him? What kind of God is he? Does God usually drop people and lose interest in them?

Praise Where Praise Is Due

"I do not cease to give thanks for you" (Eph. 1:16). Paul is not being diplomatic but simply telling the truth. He constantly praises God for the Ephesians.

How important is it that he should do so? To give thanks for a fellow believer is important for at least two reasons. In the first place God deserves to be praised for his creation. He has taken interest in someone who never merited it. He wooed a man with his Holy Spirit, brought a thousand small circumstances to bear on the man's life, preparing him to see his sin and the grace of God toward him. He cleansed him, quickened him, adopted him as his son. Even if only one man were to exist with whom God took such pains, it would be the duty of all of us to praise and thank him for such amazing kindness.

But there is a second reason why we should give thanks. We cannot give thanks and remain the same. Our perspective changes as we open our minds to God through prayer. Hope is quickened. Is the person we pray for a difficult case? If so, are we perhaps focusing on the difficulties rather than on the God of difficulties, on what has not been done rather than on what has been done?

Begin your prayer with thanksgiving. Thank God that he reached down from heaven to seize the one for whom you pray. Thank him for any evidence, past or present, of his work. Thank him for his unchanging purposes toward the person you pray for. Only when you have done so will you begin to see things in a proper light.

Something else will happen to you. You will stop praying from the darkness of your own shadow. You cannot have liberty in prayer while you are obsessed with your shadow's blackness. Huge and menacing it flickers on the wall before you, accuses you of your unfitness to pray, of your incompetence, of your unbelief. And as you shrink smaller your shadow grows larger and blacker. So give thanks. Shadows are only shadows.

Prayer deals with realities—a real God that can hear; a historical triumph on the cross witnessed by an empty tomb; a living High Priest who pleads before the throne of God; true miracles the Spirit has already brought to pass in the life of the person you pray for; a Spirit who is still present, striving to work in his or her heart. Thank him for all these things every time you pray. Fix your mind on realities and the shadows will fade away. Give God thanks and praise. He is straining to hear what you say.

Smashing Carnival Mirrors

What requests did Paul make for his Ephesian friends (Eph. 1:17-21)? Pause a moment. You are writing a letter to a friend for whom you pray fairly regularly. What will you tell him? "I do pray for you, Jack. I'm asking God to bless you and to lead you. I really pray. I pray he'll bless you richly."

What do the words mean? What does *bless* mean? Is the word an excuse on your part for not being specific? Is it too much trouble to think out a specific request? It is easier of course if Jack has pneumonia or if Jack's girl friend has just been killed in a car accident. You can get your teeth into prayer under such circumstances. But if nothing dramatic is happening to Jack and if he's a Christian who's getting along reasonably well in his Christian walk, how are you supposed to pray? *Bless* comes in handy. You probably use it at different times to mean such things as, "Do whatever is best for Jack and make things work out for him. Make him a better Christian in some way or another. Make him happy," and so on.

Are these the things God wants for Jack? What does God want? Remember God has his own goals for Jack's life. God will share those goals with you if you are willing to get involved with him in a partnership of prayer. You may need to begin praying something like this, "Lord, I don't know how to pray for Jack. I thank you for bringing him to yourself. I know you have been working in his life. What is it he most needs? What are you trying to do in him?" God still has the initiative in Jack's life. Play it God's way. That is what partnership in prayer is all about.

God's goals may differ widely from your own. To understand what goals are important to God notice the precise requests that Paul makes for the Ephesians. They are rather wordy requests and it is not easy at first to sort out their meaning. Take this long phrase for example: "that the God . . . may give you a spirit of wisdom and of revelation in the knowledge of him, having the eyes of your hearts enlightened, that you may know. . . ." If you examine it carefully, you will see that though it may sound complicated it is not vague. Paul is asking for something precise and definite. We Christians are visually handicapped. Our perspective is distorted. Bombarded from all sides with false values, living perpetually among people whose goals are material prosperity, security, pleasure, prestige, it is inevitable that we absorb the atmosphere around us until heaven seems remote while the here and now looms large in our thinking. The future comes to mean tomorrow, next week, ten years from now. We are like people looking at curved mirrors in a fun house, but unlike the crowd laughing at the grotesque images, we see the grotesque as normal! It does not amuse us. We base our lives on it.

Paul's prayer for the Ephesians is as vital for Western churches as it was for Ephesian Christians. The distorted mirrors must be smashed and replaced with straight ones. We need to see as God sees. A supernatural work of the Holy Spirit must be done in our hearts and scales swept from our eyes so that we may see.

And what is it we need to see? Three things are mentioned: the hope that lies ahead for us, our value to God, and the extraordinary power at our disposal (Eph. 1:18-19).

Our hope is to participate in Christ's ultimate triumph. It is to experience immortality and to be clothed with life. Evil is to be overthrown, judged and done away with. At present, looking at life through our crazy mirrors it seems to us that things will never change or that if they do, they will change for the worse. The here and now overwhelm us. Our jobs, our studies, our problems, the prospect of a World War 3 all crowd out the true horizon.

But for Christians the future means more than tomorrow or ten years hence, for Christ is coming back. Behind the apparent confusion there is an ordered plan, a plan in which we have a part but which is directed by the One who sits at God's right hand. We will judge angels and presidents and administer a new universal order. So will the friend we pray for. We all need to have our eyes opened to hope, the hope God called us to.

But notice I am using *hope* to mean "certainty." Hope in Scripture refers to future events that will happen come what may. Hope is not a delusion to buoy our spirits and keep us going forward blindly to an inevitable fate. It is the basis of all Christian living. It represents ultimate reality, for the Christian is to be a realist. But to live as a Christian, we must be awakened to reality. Perhaps you need such an awakening yourself. If so, I pray for you what Paul prayed for the Ephesians so that you can in turn pray the same prayer for your friends: that God will open your eyes to the glorious hope that lies ahead of you, a hope before which the importance of crises (personal or international) lessens.

Jack Is God's Treasure
Jack is one of God's jewels. Does the statement surprise you? You have seen him perhaps as "a real nice guy" or "a great Christian." Neither of these things makes him something God prizes.

He is precious to God because of God's investment in him. If you were to realize this when you prayed for Jack, I suspect your prayer would flow more easily. Part of your trouble may be that you are not really aware of how very important Jack is to God, how lively and keen God's interest is in him. Remember the parable of the Good Shepherd? It is to teach us that God has feelings about people. He has feelings about Jack. Jack is important to him, so important that Paul speaks of Jack along with the Ephesians and the rest of us as "his glorious inheritance."

Why should this be so? What is it about Jack and the rest of us that makes us such a prize to God? The thesis of Milton's *Paradise Lost* is that Satan knew the thing he could do to hurt God most was to cause people to fall into sin, so great was God's delight in humanity.

Two reasons account for God's delight. Unique in his creation, human beings alone were made in God's image. Among all that was ever created humans most nearly resemble God. If we are wrecks, we are wrecks of something very noble.

But Jack is more than a noble wreck because a further divine investment has been made in him. God sent his Son, born of a woman, to restore his image in Jack. And while Jack may not impress you very much, God views him with different eyes. God does not treasure galaxies. He treasures people, especially redeemed people, rescued from sin at the price of blood. Jack is part of God's "glorious inheritance," so that when you pray for Jack you are praying for no ordinary person. Whereas you may see a round-shouldered youth with acne and a slouch, God sees incomparable treasure. Remember that when you pray.

But remember something else. Jack needs to know how God feels toward him. You must pray that Jack's eyes be opened too. Once it dawns on him that he is infinitely precious to God, his own outlook on life will change. He will feel different about himself, will hold his head higher without ceasing to be humble. He will find it easier to enter God's presence. Such will be the change in him that you and your friends will notice it.

The Seal of Power
Our destinies seem to be decided in Washington, Moscow, Peking, in air-conditioned offices of multinational corporations or in the club rooms of the power elite. What power do we have over our own or other people's lives? Democracy is good, but how can Jack's one vote change his own or anyone else's destiny?

Paul prays that the Ephesians will realize the power at work in them. In answer to our query as to what power and how much, we are told, "the immeasurable greatness of [God's] power" (Eph. 1:19). Moscow? Washington? How does their power compare with the immeasurable greatness of God's power? Does God not hold presidents, cartels and the editor of the Washington Post in the palm of his hand on a tiny spinning sphere?

Our eyes need to be opened to this fact too. Two thousand years ago the disciples' eyes were opened briefly as the immeasurable power of God gently removed a stone from a cave and raised the Son to resurrection life. No corporation or government could do that. And now enthroned above all universes, all gods, dominions, devils, hierarchies, potentates sits the risen, exalted Christ.

It is important to understand that we are not talking empty theology but everyday reality. All this power, this immeasurably great power, is *in* believers (Eph. 1:19). The problem is that most believers do not really grasp it. Their eyes need to be opened not only to the hope awaiting them and the love of God toward them, but to the power at work within them. One glimpse of the great power would revolutionize us all. We don't use it because we don't see it. Sometimes we do not see it because we dare not see it.

You can see, can't you, Paul's strategy in prayer? Most of us, when we are not hung up with the word "bless," get bogged down with trivia: Jane's sinus trouble, Ben's discouragement, Mary's problem with her mother-in-law, the pastor's prostate operation. All of these may be important, but prayer, like warfare, calls for strategy.

It is said of Napoleon that he would watch the development of his battles from a vantage, quietly analyzing the situation while he watched. His key general would watch with him. "That farm," he once said to Marshal Ney, "that farm that you can see on the ridge there. Take it. Seize it. Hold it. For if you can, the battle is won."

In praying for the Ephesians Paul was aware that if the key to the whole battle was won, lesser skirmishes would sort themselves out relatively easily. Smaller problems are so often symptomatic of larger issues. Intercessory prayer must be directed to that which is the key. It concerns itself with strategy, not with tactics.

If therefore one feels that Paul's prayer is spiritual and not practical, it is a sign of how blind he or she is to what life is all about. The person who knows his true destiny is to reign with Christ, whose eyes are opened to his or her true hope, the person who is keenly aware that in God's eyes he or she is exceedingly precious, the person who has caught a glimpse of the fact that the power of the universe's Creator is within him or herself, this person does not need prayer about minor or even major problems he may encounter in life. He can handle them easily.

But Paul has not finished his strategic requests for the Ephesians. Taking up his prayer in Ephesians 3:14 he amplifies the matter of power, asking that the Ephesians "be strengthened with might through his Spirit in the inner man, and that Christ may dwell in [their] hearts through faith."

Power in Christians is not raw energy. Rather than being a highly charged atomic source under our control, it springs from a union between us and God. God the Holy Spirit inhabits our inner beings. And since Spirit, Father and Son are one God, we may say the triune God dwells in each of us. The raw power belongs to us. It is limitless, incalculable, inexpressible. *It* is in Jack because *they* are in Jack.

Yet there seems to be a catch. Paul prays "that Christ may dwell in your hearts through faith." Does Christ not dwell there anyway? If Jack is a Christian may he not say at any time, "Christ, by his Spirit, lives in my heart"? Why then should Paul pray that an already existing state of affairs be brought about?

We have already looked at the problem in part. God in his omnipotence might just as well not be present in most Christians. Compare them with their non-Christian friends and neighbors. Is it not true that while they may have a form of godliness, their very lives deny its power? What evidence of the supernatural can be seen in the average Christian Joe? Not very much. Why? Because the average Christian Joe does not believe that God is really there. His eyes have not been opened. His faith is not being exercised. To all intents and purposes Christ might just as well be an eternity away from him.

Now we cannot pray that someone else become aware of the

vast power-potential within him or her unless we are aware of it in ourselves. Our own eyes need to be opened. But we can't wait for the miracle to happen. In a practical sense Christ will dwell in our hearts when we begin to count on him to do so.

He who is there in fact, will be there in power when we start to believe it and to act accordingly. And when such a state of affairs comes about, our friends can drop a lot of their more trivial prayers for us and concentrate on praying that we continue to be "strengthened with might through his Spirit in the inner man."

The Hands of Love Reach Down
Paul has a final prayer request for the Ephesians. Clearly no prayer request could be more strategic than love since love is both what God *is* and at the same time the summum bonum in Christian experience.

Paul requests several things about love for his Ephesian friends: that they be "rooted and grounded in love" (Eph. 3:17); that they may comprehend and know its vast extent; and that in so doing they may be "filled with all the fulness of God" (Eph. 1:18-19). These are ambitious requests. There is really little left to ask once you have made the request that someone be filled with all the fullness of God.

Let us examine the requests more closely. They are, of course, interrelated and lead naturally one into the other. What is it first of all to be rooted and grounded in love? Paul wants love to be something extremely basic in the lives of the Ephesians. The question we ask must be more precise. What we need to know is whether Paul refers to our love for others or God's love for us. Paul's third request indicates to me that to be rooted and grounded in love means to live a life in which all my thoughts and actions spring from an awareness of how much *God* loves *me*.

For many years I was frightened of being loved. I did not mind *giving* love (or what I thought was love), but I grew ill

137

at ease if anyone, man, woman or child, showed too much affection for me. In our family we had never learned how to handle love. We were not very expert at demonstrating it or at receiving it. I don't mean that we did not love one another or that we did not find ways of showing it. But we were very British. When I was nineteen and leaving home to go to war, my father did something quite unprecedented. He put his hands on my shoulders and kissed me. I was stunned. I knew neither what to say nor what to do. For me it was embarrassing while for my father it must have been very sad.

But the matter went deeper. For years I realized intellectually that Christ loved me, but I did not want him to come too close with his love. I wanted to follow him and was willing (I think) to die for him if necessary. *I* loved *him*. Sometimes I could express my love to him fervently in prayer. But at the same time I was scared of his love getting too close to me.

One day I had a vision, a real one in three dimensions and full color. I was praying with friends at the time and was acutely conscious of my particular problem, my fear of being loved. Gradually I became aware that the hands of Christ were outstretched toward me a little distance away, in front of me and above me. They didn't just appear. It was as though they had been there always but that I had never really paid attention to them before. I noticed the nail prints. While I was fully aware that what I saw was a mental phenomenon, I found myself sweating profusely and trembling. Tears ran down my cheeks.

The hands were outstretched as if to invite me to take hold of them, yet my arms hung like lead by my sides. With all my heart I wanted to reach up, but I was powerless. Beneath my fear of love was a still deeper longing to be loved, to know I was loved, to receive love. The vision and my helplessness symbolized my inner problem. I wept bitterly. "O Lord, I want to grasp your hands." Over and over I repeated the words, "But I can't." Slowly the vision receded into the back of my mind, and in the quietness that followed, there came to me an assurance that the defensive wall I had built around me would gradually be dismantled and that I would learn what it was to let Christ's love wrap around me and fill me.

And thus it has proved, gradually changing my life so that now, in some degree at least, I am "rooted and grounded in love." My life is founded on love, the love of Christ toward me. My roots draw nourishment from that love.

I do not know the means by which the Holy Spirit teaches others what it is to be rooted and grounded in love. Yet the Christ who loves does not love passively. By one means or another he seeks to reach us with love. On your part your faith is more important than perceiving any visions. Believe when you pray that the Christ who dwells within you is a Christ who loves you as no one else has or ever will. Nothing in you, in earth or in hell can stop him loving you. And as you pray for Jack, pray that he too may be "rooted and grounded" in love as he perceives how greatly he is loved.

In knowing the love that passes knowledge we are changed. And to know it involves, in some degree at least, comprehending it. But who can grasp what so vast a love is?

The apostle is praying no ideal, impossible prayer. The Ephesians are to understand "with all the saints" what the love of Christ is. All Christians are meant to grasp it, not to understand an abstract concept but to perceive that they themselves are loved by a love that has no measure.

I get the feeling that Paul, as he reduces his thoughts to language, has to struggle to contain powerfully explosive concepts in such fragile vessels as words. Or perhaps he is aware of the limitations in the thinking of the Ephesians and finds it hard to bridge the wide gap between what is and what they perceive. Yet as I mentioned a few sentences back, the prayer is intensely practical and is meant to be answered. It is the will of God that all Christians be made aware of the love Paul speaks of and to have their eyes opened to the power of the triune God within them.

If you find it hard to believe this, read the verse that follows Paul's prayer. Write it out and tape it to the wall above your bed. Perhaps it will stimulate your faith as you read, "Now to him who by the power at work within us is able to do far more abundantly than all that we ask or think . . ."

10

Then Jesus went with them to a place called Gethsemane, and he said to his disciples, "Sit here, while I
go yonder and pray." And taking with him Peter and
the two sons of Zebedee, he began to be sorrowful and
troubled. Then he said to them, "My soul is very sorrowful, even to death; remain here, and watch with
me." And going a little farther he fell on his face and
prayed, "My Father, if it be possible, let this cup pass
from me; nevertheless, not as I will, but as thou wilt."
And he came to the disciples and found them sleeping;
and he said to Peter, "So, could you not watch with me
one hour? Watch and pray that you may not enter
into temptation; the spirit indeed is willing, but the
flesh is weak." Again, for the second time, he went
away and prayed, "My Father, if this cannot pass
unless I drink it, thy will be done." And again he came
and found them sleeping, for their eyes were heavy. So,
leaving them again, he went away and prayed for the
third time, saying the same words. Then he came to the
disciples and said to them, "Are you still sleeping and
taking your rest? Behold, the hour is at hand, and the
Son of man is betrayed into the hands of sinners. Rise,
let us be going; see, my betrayer is at hand." . . . Now
from the sixth hour there was darkness over all the
land until the ninth hour. And about the ninth hour
Jesus cried with a loud voice, "Eli, Eli, lama sabach-
thani?" that is, "My God, my God, why hast thou forsaken me?"

And Jesus said, "Father, forgive them; for they know
not what they do." . . . Then Jesus, crying with a loud
voice, said, "Father, into thy hands I commit my
spirit!" And having said this he breathed his last.

JESUS:
THE LAST BATTLE

LET US TREAD SOFTLY for we walk on holy ground. We have, as a matter of fact, been doing so all along since it is no light matter to breathe over a man's shoulder as he bows in the presence of his Maker. But as we approach the Son of man in prayer a new solemnity is called for.

I propose to discuss reverently the last known prayers of Jesus Christ. One was protracted and uttered under extreme emotional stress. Three others, ejaculatory, were spoken at a time when physical agony and exhaustion complicated that same stress.

I feel presumptuous adding to what has already been written. Yet I am drawn powerfully to the scenes where the prayers were uttered, and I invite you to watch and listen with me. I think I can say that the invitation comes from God rather than from me. If such solemn scenes are described and such solemn words recorded, it follows that we must all watch and listen whether we would like to or not. Only let us do so with our hearts bowed.

People in Prayer

A Yearning for Companionship

We are observing the Son of God as he addresses the Father. More importantly we are seeing a man, the Son of man, approaching the Father of us all. And it is as man that I want us to observe him most. We cannot identify with his deity. But in humanity we are bound together with him and he with us.

The scene in the garden is well known. The eleven disciples accompanied him to the Mount of Olives and were instructed to pray "that you may not enter into temptation." A comparison of the accounts in the different Gospels reveals that he went on further, "about a stone's throw," (Lk. 22:41) taking with him Peter, James and John, and speaking with them beyond the hearing of the rest. Evidently the four sat down together briefly, and in the heavy silence that followed the disciples were able to observe Christ's agitation and distress (Mt. 26:37).

The fact that he asked for their company, that he told them his soul was deeply troubled, "even to death," the fact that he requested them to remain sitting with him, waiting for him as he continued a few paces further to pray, indicates his human need for company and support. In the loneliness of their responsibilities, leaders experience times when the yearning for human understanding and support can be almost unbearable. If you should be in a position of Christian leadership, take heart. The Son of man himself knew that same yearning. He could not share fully the awful thing that lay heavily upon his heart, yet clearly he reached out for support from the three men nearest to him. There are times for all of us to do the same.

We, of course, need never be bereft of divine support. Jesus, on the night of his betrayal, was in a more terrible position. He faced the loss of the very relationship that gave him the strength to be the leader he was. The time was approaching when intimacy with his Father was to exist no longer. Heaven would be black and silent. The Father would turn his back. We crave human support because we have never truly learned to rest in God. He craved it because divine support was to be taken away.

The three must have heard some of his prayer for the key words must have been to the disciples what the earnest talk of adults is to children. Children, while they may be oppressed by emotion, fail to follow the nuances of meaning. They are out of their depth. Matters beyond their capacity to respond trouble their hearts and confuse their minds. In the same way the disciples could not keep pace with the battle in his soul. Sleep overwhelmed them.

The Storm Subsides

Meanwhile for Jesus the issues narrowed down to one. Was there no other way? Could not some way be found that would avoid the limitless blackness that was to engulf his soul? If not, he would go forward. But surely some other way must exist.

How wonderful that God became a man! How amazing that Jesus grappled with an issue we grapple with ourselves. "I'll do it Lord, if that's really what you want. But I don't know how I can. Is this really what you want me to face?"

One may say we have no right to compare our small dilemmas with his great one. Yet why not? Is not the whole point that he trod the road of deepest perplexity ahead of us? To be sure we have no dilemma like his, no Gethsemane, no horror of such blackness. Yet with mingled sorrow and gladness we may watch him as the disciples sleep, and see that we have a High Priest who can be touched by the feelings of our own weaknesses. He has passed that way himself.

Jesus the Son of man did not find it easy to say, "Not as I will, but as thou wilt" (Mt. 26:39). He was down on his face when he said it. Later manuscripts add what earlier manuscripts omit, "And being in an agony he prayed more earnestly; and his sweat became like great drops of blood falling down upon the ground" (Lk. 22:44). The words are fully commensurate with the pain. It went against every human instinct of survival, against every spiritual, God-implanted longing in his human being to face death and sin-caused alienation from God the Father. Body and soul cried out against it, so that in the teeth of an inner storm of protest he had to say with his naked will, "Not as I will, but as thou wilt."

He said the words by faith. He knew by faith, not by feeling, that the Father was just, omnipotent and trustworthy. But Jesus was human as well as divine, and his body was in revolt against all he was called on to face.

After an hour or so there may have been a measure of peace in his soul. He would go forward to death if he had to. The rough earth would be pressing against his body, and he would rise stiffly to walk over to his supporters where they were sleeping. It was a measure of his growing strength that as he woke them he was now able to minister to their weakness, being sufficiently free from his own preoccupation to see them as he usually saw them, weak and in need of counsel.

The story of all that follows is well known. Twice more he returned to grapple in prayer with the issue before him. Why?

Evidently the storms within him did not abate at once. Again they broke out threatening in their fury to sweep his resolve away. Is not this our experience too? When God calls for a course which our nature cries out against, we may know from the outset that the course is a right one. But storms do not abate simply because the helmsman decides to maintain course. Nor as waves come washing over the decks or the chart grows wet and crumpled does the captain cease to check the rightness of that course.

How hard I have found it at times to keep my prow into the wind. I battle with will and wits against wind and water. When the sails crack angrily and sheet and tiller tug powerfully as if to wrest themselves from my grasp, I find myself saying again, "Is there not some other way to do this?" But sometimes there is not. And grimly I must hold onto my course, whatever the storm may threaten.

Let it not dismay you then that in the fiercest storms of life the wind and waves should continue to buffet you long after you have said, "Not my will, but yours, O Lord!" The storm will not last forever. But it need not abate the moment you set your course.

For Jesus the inner storm eventually died down. With quietness of soul and firm resolve he woke his little band while the lights of his captors flickered slowly up the hillside. Standing with his sleepy disciples he waited in perfect composure for all that was to follow.

"Father, Forgive Them."

Spikes had been driven through wrists and ankles. The stake bearing his shocked and dehydrated body had been dropped with a thud into a hole prepared for it. Callous soldiers were already sorting out his clothing to divide among themselves.

The unselfishness of his prayer "Father, forgive them . . ." is what arrests us. We know that in physical pain we ourselves grow self-centered, asking for sympathy in subtle or not-so-subtle ways. Similarly when we face injustice or cold lack of consideration from our fellows, we are absorbed with the way we are being treated. Resentment, rage, bitterness and self-pity among other feelings, vie for center stage in our attention. We become wrapped in our pain, our misery, our bitterness.

Yet here is someone whose capacity to drop such feelings like a cloak excites our amazement. His physical sufferings alone were great. Having been lashed with lead-tipped thongs until skin, fat and muscle were ripped from his back, having lost body fluids, electrolytes and sweat under a hot sun, he had approached his final hours of agony with a weakened, pain-wracked frame.

The unique torture of crucifixion lies in its sadistic offer of a choice between two horrors. To hang with arms out-stretched for hours induces cramps in the muscles of chest, abdomen and diaphragm. Breathing becomes labored and painful and suffocation threatens. Yet to fill one's lungs with air demands that one raise one's body by transferring its weight to the spike through the ankles and to struggle to hang less and raise oneself more. When the pain becomes unbearable, one may sink down to cramps and suffocation again.

The physical agony might obliterate all else for some people. But a hardier soul is conscious of the morbid interest of the crowds, the jeers and most painful of all, the dividing up of the bits and pieces—the robe, the sandals that connect him with the world of living people and now symbolically seal his dismissal from them.

There is no doubt that a man who can so quickly drop his self-absorption, his concentration on intense physical suffering, his temptation to rage, resentment, hate, self-pity so that he can be interested in, understand, let alone forgive his tormentors, is a man who merits our supreme admiration. To call on God at such a moment, under such circumstances, to rise above all that would drag him down and pray, "Father, forgive them; for they know not what they do," leaves us spellbound with wonder.

And he calls us to follow him, to follow him, that is, in his amazing capacity to ignore the demands of his bodily and emotional needs and be concerned with others. The pathway is uninviting, impossibly steep, but rewarding. We cannot climb it without divine aid.

You will say, "But my bodily and emotional needs have to be met somehow." Indeed they do. Yet when you are overwhelmed with sadness there are two kinds of help you can receive. One person's reaction to your sorrow will leave you wallowing in self-pity, your arms hanging loosely and your brooding eyes on the floor. Your friend may be solicitous, too solicitous. He may merely deepen your attitude of sorrow by subtly magnifying your right to be miserable. You will have sung the pitiful duet of, "I will moan for you and you can sigh for me." Another friend may respond sympathetically yet leave you refreshed and strengthened. You will be satisfied. You know you have been understood and cared for, and now you are free to forget your sorrows.

God offers this second kind of help. He gives a sympathy that strengthens, refreshes, renews. Again I must emphasize that no sorrows you or I experience could compare with the sufferings of Christ. But that is not my purpose. We are called to look on and emulate him who thought of others while he was in pain. There will always be grace available if we want to do so.

But there is a deeper lesson in the forgiveness prayer. Christ shows more than a capacity to transcend pain and show concern for others. That much could be seen in his concern for his mother Mary's well-being (Jn. 19:25-26). The matter goes further. He pleads forgiveness for personal wrong done against him. We are called to follow in his pathway of forgiveness.

You must notice, of course, that we are dealing with prayer for the forgiveness of others. It is a kind of prayer we rarely make use of. Are you critical of someone? It matters little whether they have used you ill or whether their sin affects someone else. If the wrong has been done to you, your criticism doubtless will be mingled with resentment. It may seem that the heart of the battle lies precisely here—with your feelings of criticism and resentment.

You are, let us suppose, a fairly "mature" Christian. You know perfectly well that forgiveness is a must. Yet you battle constantly with resentment. It is all made worse because the person you contend with refuses (or is unable) to change his ways. He constantly makes the same mistakes, treads on the same sore toe.

Stop grappling with your feelings. Raise the issue to an altogether higher level. Go to the Father and pray that the Father will forgive. "Lord, forgive Joe. You have forgiven me, and you have forgiven many who have done greater wrongs than Joe. Forgive him, Father. He probably doesn't realize what he's doing."

I am perfectly serious about the matter, and you must be too. God will in fact take you seriously when you pray for the forgiveness of another. The capacity to pray in this way is what makes you a priest. You are to follow in the steps of the High Priest and to plead for mercy for those who need it. In doing so you will transcend that form of forgiveness which merely affects the horizontal relationship between you and a fellow creature, and will be calling for divine forgiveness of sin from the only Source able to provide that forgiveness.

The results may surprise you. Changes in your attitude and in your friend's behavior are both likely to follow for you will not have been playing with words. You will have exercised a valid priestly function affirmed at the time of the Protestant Reformation and largely forgotten except in words.

What holds you back from starting? Do you feel I am asking too much? But it is not I who ask. Look, if you can, at the man whose body is being raised up on a gibbet, whose clothes are being divided up. It is no hollow display of piety that comes from his lips. He knows exactly what he is asking and he asks it because he wants the forgiveness to be given. He it is who calls you to follow him, in this manner, along this pathway.

Forsaken

No more horrifying prayer ever burst from a human mouth: "My God, my God, why hast thou forsaken me?" The words resonate chillingly in our minds because of the person who uttered them and because of the fate they speak of.

We all dread abandonment. No abandonment could be worse than abandonment by God. It is ultimate forsakenness. It is death and hell in experience.

The One who cried out ought never to have been abandoned. It is horrendous, unthinkable that he should be. But we are horrified partly because we know the unthinkable spells out our own guilt. This cosmic havoc is our doing and we are appalled as we see what ruin we are capable of.

But we must quell our terror. What seems to be havoc is the birth of something new. This ruin we can no longer control is, paradoxically, the work of Almighty Justice restoring order and peace. The process may be terrible, but it is good and will produce good.

Let us then not look at that which is unspeakable, but at that which was spoken: "My God . . . why?" For him it was legitimate to use the word. We would never dare question that Christ should so pray in such circumstances. The words may be terrible, but they are appropriate. Yet when you or I find ourselves praying, "My God . . . why?" there are those who instantly rise up to rebuke us. One must not question God.

I said at the beginning of the chapter that we are treading on holy ground. A comparison of our own distresses with Christ's great distress seems presumptuous and distasteful. But the point at issue lies neither in the relative quantities of our suffering (such comparisons certainly being odious) nor in their quality (there being no redemptive component in our suffering). Rather it lies in the fact that we are called to follow Christ, that the servant is not greater than his Lord, that the same kind of dilemma the Savior faced will be faced by his followers.

If I were coldly logical I could point out that Jesus knew the answer to his own agonized cry. *He knew why.* He had known during his earthly ministry. He had known with awful clarity in the Mount of Olives. His question is not a plea for intellectual understanding but an expression of agony that overwhelmed understanding.

And while none of us will ever face what our Lord faced, we may find ourselves, even though we too know the answer to our own question, still crying, "Why?" We cry because our natures protest what is happening to us. We understand yet we do not understand, just as a nonswimmer "understands" that his body is lighter than water until he is thrown into a lake. So we struggle in desperation while the waters swirl round our souls, and the knowledge we possess seems powerless to prevent us from drowning.

It is far better to cry "Why?" than not to cry at all. It is better to protest in dismay than to curse God and die. Implicit in the question "Why?" is a belief that someone exists who can hear and answer us. Our very agitation is a product of faith; faltering faith perhaps, but faith nonetheless. Once we lose all hope that there is an ear to hear or a heart that is concerned, despair becomes absolute. Agitation subsides leaving us waiting quietly for doom to come.

But Christ is asking a specific "Why?" It is not, "Why do I suffer?" but "Why have you abandoned me?" Why have you closed your ears and shut your eyes? Why does my plight fail to move you? Why am I cut off? Why the silence and the darkness?

If there is one thing Jesus as man could be sure of in his relationship with the Father, it was of the Father's trustworthiness. Those who were the Father's would never be forsaken. Jesus had committed himself to the risks and the humiliations of becoming a human infant, of facing hunger, pain, persecution, misunderstanding, physical weakness and demonic attack, knowing that his Father could be trusted never to fail him. His faith in the Father had been unwavering, his communion with him constant and absolute.

Now suddenly he has no more assurance. Communion is dead. He is in blackness. The impossible has happened. The Father has indeed forsaken him, and the abandonment is total. It is useless for him to appeal for deliverance for the Father will no longer pay heed. A Father the Son of Man never knew has sprung into being. Jesus encounters hostility in place of acceptance, cold rage in place of gentleness, implacable hatred instead of love.

> Jehovah bade his sword awake:
>   O Christ, it woke 'gainst thee;
> Thy blood the flaming blade must slake,
>   Thy heart its sheath must be,
> All for my sake, my peace to make:
>   Now sleeps that sword for me.
> (Anne Ross Cousin, "O Christ, What Burdens Bowed Thy
>   Head.")

We are not at this point dealing with theology but with experience, and in particular with what Jesus experienced as a man. Why he experienced it is ably dealt with elsewhere. The fact is that he did. And it is from the horror of this very experience that he cried out, "My God, my God, why hast thou forsaken me?"

You too, for altogether different reasons, may one day feel you are undergoing a similar experience. An ancient writer expressed himself eloquently when he wrote:

> I am the man who has seen affliction under the rod of his
>   wrath;
> he has driven and brought me
>   into darkness without any light;
> surely against me he turns his hand
>   again and again the whole day long.
>
> He has made my flesh and my skin waste away,
>   and broken my bones;
> he has besieged and enveloped me
>   with bitterness and tribulation;
> he has made me dwell in darkness
>   like the dead of long ago.
>
> He has walled me about so that I cannot escape;
>   he has put heavy chains on me;

> though I call and cry for help,
>   he shuts out my prayer;
> he has blocked my ways with hewn stones,
>   he has made my paths crooked.
>
> He is to me like a bear lying in wait,
>   like a lion in hiding;
> he led me off my way and tore me to pieces;
>   he has made me desolate;
> he bent his bow and set me
>   as a mark for his arrow.
>
> He drove into my heart
>   the arrows of his quiver;
> I have become the laughingstock of all peoples,
>   the burden of their songs all day long.
> He has filled me with bitterness,
>   he has sated me with wormwood.
>
> He has made my teeth grind on gravel,
>   and made me cower in ashes;
> my soul is bereft of peace,
>   I have forgotten what happiness is;
> so I say, "Gone is my glory,
>   and my expectation from the LORD." (Lam. 3:1-18)

Should you encounter such an experience there are a number of things you must bear in mind. It is not wrong to cry in bewilderment to God. He listened to Job, he will listen to you. The darkness may not immediately lessen, but to cry out is natural and altogether appropriate. He waits, tenderly and patiently to hear you cry, "Oh God, where are you?" He knows then what you still expect of him.

But the most important point to grasp is that you will not be the first to tread so dark a valley, to feel so alone, so alienated from God. There is someone who has trodden it be-

fore you. And the valley will end. Calvary was followed by a
tearing aside of all that hid God, by a bursting from the tomb
and by ascension to glory. The glory that is to be revealed in
you will shine the brighter against the blackness from which
you will emerge.

The Last Prayer

Jesus emerged from the blackness before he died. He did not
have to wait for an open tomb and a resurrection body. The
face of his Father shone lovingly upon him again on *this* side
of the grave. Darkness may still have covered the land. The
fearful rending of the "veil of the temple" might intimidate
any who saw it. But for Jesus the battle was ended.

Suddenly there was no sign of his bodily weakness. Pain
was vanquished, sorrow ended and bewilderment gone.
Across the dark valley and over the heads of the watching
crowd his voice rang out powerfully, joyfully, "Father, into
thy hands I commit my spirit!" And so he died.

His words have assumed all the characteristics of a legend.
I do not mean they were not spoken, for they were; indeed
they burst from his lungs with a ringing joy. But we have
learned to treat them as legend. For us they are the lines of a
Bach cantata, solemnly ornamental, fitting, beautiful, but removed from our daily reality. We treat them as a masterpiece
in religious art.

We deepen our isolation from the prayer by talking non-
sense about it. Jesus, we say, had the power to dismiss his
spirit; we do not. Therefore the prayer is special to Jesus and
bears no relationship to our own lives. It is for Good Friday,
sad faces and solemn music.

People in primitive areas still know the day and hour of
their dying. Many of us in the West will know, if not the precise moment, at least the fact that the death process is upon
us. Certainly the patriarchs all knew when they were dying.
Therefore the prayer of Jesus must not be regarded as some-

thing peculiar to his redemptive work. He was showing us how to die. He was dying in the proper manner, dying the death of a believer, praying the final prayer as it ought to be prayed.

Does it seem strange to you that I should try to teach you how to die? Am I, perhaps, getting things out of proportion? Isn't Christianity for *living*? Yet dying is part of living, therefore Christian dying is as important as Christian living. The shelves of your local Christian bookstore are crammed with books telling you how to live a Christian life, but I'll wager you'll search long and hard before you find one telling you how to die a Christian death. You don't wish to think about dying? But why not? Is dying something a Christian should avoid or be afraid of?

To be sure an untimely death is to be prayed against. Death that comes on us before it should is tragedy. Yet the man or woman who lives for God need have no fear of untimely death. Such a person, in the words of the popular expression, is immortal until his work is completed.

The whole trouble about our attitude to death is that we concentrate on what is to happen to us rather than on what we should be doing. We are subject to fear because our eyes are in the wrong direction. We look at what we cannot control rather than at what we can.

In myth and cartoon the Man with the Scythe comes for us at the appointed hour. We tremble and shrink back. To every last second we cling in panic, all the time knowing we cannot resist the Reaper who comes. We shrivel inside ourselves and our hearts stop beating from very fear.

It makes a world of difference when you know what you have to do in any circumstance. To have a plan, to be trained to act will change your outlook totally. Panic and fear are the companions of passivity.

When the first airraid sirens woke me as a boy, I was not afraid because I knew exactly what to do. I got up, dressed (suit, collar and tie), woke the rest of the family and joined them in the airraid shelter. Once we were there we each had our little chores to do and special points to remember. I do not possess outstanding courage. My fear was substantially reduced because I knew how I was supposed to behave. I was not a helpless, passive victim but an active participant in a plan.

As a Christian you must not be a passive, cringing victim of death. Your attitude must be what Christ's was and the core of his attitude is found in his final prayer. Should you be vaporized in an atomic holocaust you may not have time to take action or to adopt attitudes. But there is a strong possibility that you will face death with your eyes open. What will you do? What attitude will you adopt?

We must confine ourselves to the heart of the matter, to what Christ prayed and how he prayed it. "Into thy hands I commit my spirit!" The prayer is a prayer of faith. He did not say, "Into thy hands I hope my spirit will eventually drift," but instead he made a declaration of firm trust. It was, in fact, more than a declaration. It was a commitment.

Death involves a choice. We cannot at the end choose whether we die, but we may choose how to do so. We may choose for instance whether we bear witness with joy to our faith in God or whether we are dragged off-stage.

For in life we are on a stage. The audience is both human and ghostly. Angels and demons watch as we enact the drama of our earthly existence, and it is important that the scene close properly. A brilliant opening act can be spoiled by a feeble ending. Christ has shown us how the lines should be uttered, as a cry of joyful triumph. "Father, into thy hands I commit my spirit!" You will only die once and will only therefore have one chance of dying properly. There will be no rehearsals for most of us. Learn your lines well beforehand so that the curtains fall on a note of triumph.

You may wonder how it is that Jesus did not say, "Father into thy hands I commend my *body*." For it was in the body he had lived, suffered and been tormented. It was his body that was being left behind, and from Scripture it is plain that his body was much more than the cast-off clothing of his spirit. We are not dealing with the chrysalis case a butterfly leaves behind. Instead this is a body in which decomposition, however effectively delayed, was to begin before its arrest at the resurrection. If he should show concern, why did he not show it with his body, rather than his spirit?

We are not bodies. We *have* bodies. To be sure, it is clear from Scripture that both here and hereafter we shall never cease to be bodily creatures. Our bodies, like his, will be changed and renewed so that throughout eternity spirit and body will be united. Each of us will be a *new* human but still human.

Yet to those of us who are living, it is hard to conceive that the preoccupation of the dying should be with the spirit rather than with the body. Some of us at least have a morbid preoccupation with the ugly decomposition or the horrifying frying of the most intimate possession we have. How can its molecules be brought together again? How can decay be arrested, reversed, transformed?

Is it not precisely here where most of our present doubts and fears center? For whatever we believe in our heads, the only life we have ever experienced is bodily life. And if our bodies are to be eaten by worms, what will become of us? Uncomfortably we struggle to suppress the fear that death in the end may digest us all back into the material universe.

Yet at the time of death a different fear can arise. Suddenly a man becomes aware that in a moment there will be no clothing for his spirit. Stark naked it will face the fiery, icy blasts of eternity with no body to shelter it. A man whose clothes are torn from him does not think about whether he will ever get his jacket back but about how he can face life so uncovered. It is his nakedness that discomfits him.

Oh, how shall I, whose native sphere
    Is dark, whose mind is dim,

Before th' Ineffable appear,
And on my naked spirit bear
The uncreated beam?
(T. Binny, "Eternal Light! Eternal Light!")

In the light of such fears the words of Jesus make sense. It is in the *spirit* alone that he will storm the gates of hell to declare his triumph over death and sin. Spirit and body are temporarily to be separated and what he faces is the sudden stripping away of that body from the personal spirit of Jesus the man. (For Jesus was not merely God inside a body. While remaining God, he *became* man, assuming not only man's outward form but his inward personality.)

When you face death, then, it is this that you will face, not the dissolution of your body, but its being stripped (for repair and renewal) from your spirit.

Do not let the nakedness make you afraid. The God who breathed into your nostrils the breath of life, who also redeemed you and plans to clothe you with immortality will be there to receive you personally in the wings. The curtain may fall and your bodily costume taken (temporarily) from you, but you can walk with confidence toward your Maker and Redeemer saying in triumph, "Here is my spirit. Take it, it is yours. Clothe it again when you are ready. Into your arms I gladly bring it."

John Donne, metaphysical poet and Dean of St. Paul's Cathedral, London, whose seventeenth-century English still affects our everyday speech with such well-known phrases as "for whom the bell tolls" and "no man is an island" is best known for his own extraordinary valor in the face of death. Shortly before his death, he got out of bed to preach in St. Paul's his last, and what was at the time generally agreed to be his own funeral sermon entitled "Death's Duel." His chosen text was Psalm 68:20, "And to God, the Lord, belongs escape from death." Returning to bed, he composed the following hymn:

159

People in Prayer

Since I am comming to that Holy roome,
  Where, with thy Quire of Saints for evermore,
I shall be made thy Musique; As I come
  I tune the Instrument here at the dore,
  And what I must doe then, thinke here before.

... As the first *Adams* sweat surrounds my face,
  May the last *Adams* blood my soule embrace.

So, in his purple wrapp'd receive mee Lord,
  By these his thornes give me his other Crowne;
And as to other soules I preach'd thy word,
  Be this my Text, my Sermon to mine owne,
  Therefore that he may raise the Lord throws down.
("Hymne to God my God, in my Sicknesse," *John Donne, a Selection of his Poetry,* edited by John Hayward [Harmondsworth: Penguin, 1950], p. 177.)
Charles Lamb, Donne's biographer writes, "In the last hour of his last day ... his soul, having, I verily believe, some revelation of the beatific vision, he said, 'I were miserable if I might not die'; and after those words, closed many periods of his faint breath by saying often, 'Thy kingdom come, Thy will be done.' ... Seeing heaven by that illumination ... he closed his own eyes, and then disposed his hands and body into such a posture, as required not the least alteration by those who came to shroud him" (*Devotions,* p. xviii).

The play has been running a long time. You are the successor of a highly distinguished cast. The Father with the whole of the cast awaits you in the wings. Therefore let the words ring out so that they reach the furthest corners of the theater, "Father, into thy hands I commit my spirit." They will form the last prayer you utter on earth.

They will be your closing lines in Act I.